T0333244

BRUTALIST BRITAIN

BRITAIN

ELAIN HARWOOD

BATSFORD

First published in the United Kingdom in 2022 by

B. T. Batsford Ltd
43 Great Ormond Street
London
WC1N 3HZ

An imprint of B. T. Batsford Holdings Limited

Copyright © B.T. Batsford Ltd 2022
Text copyright © Elain Harwood 2022

All rights reserved. No part of this publication may be copied, displayed,
extracted, reproduced, utilized, stored in a retrieval system or transmitted
in any form or by any means, electronic, mechanical or otherwise including
but not limited to photocopying, recording, or scanning without the prior written
permission of the publishers.

ISBN 978 1 84994 727 5

A CIP catalogue record for this book is available from the British Library.

10 9 8 7 6 5 4 3 2 1

Reproduction by Rival Colour Ltd, UK
Printed and bound by Toppan Leefung Printing Ltd, China

Chapter openers: page 20 Sugden House, Watford; 1955–56 by Alison & Peter Smithson; 28 Public Housing: Dawson's
Heights, East Dulwich, London; 1968–72 by Kate Macintosh, Southwark Architect's Department; 74 Education: Essex
University Library; 1965–67 by Kenneth Capon of the Architects' Co-Partnership; 126 Public Buildings: Hove Town Hall;
1970–74 by John Wells-Thorpe; 154 Shops, Markets and Town Centres: Anglia Square, Norwich; 1966–71 by Alan Cooke
& Partners; 176 Works of Art: Henge, Beaufort Drive, Glenrothes; 1970 by David Harding; 196 Culture and Sport: Theatr
Ardudwy, Harlech, Wales; 1973–78 by Gerald Latter of Colwyn Foulkes & Partners; 238 Places of Worship: St Peter's
Seminary, Cardross, Scotland; 1962–66 by Isi Metzstein and Andy MacMillan of Gillespie, Kidd & Coia; 256 Offices and
Industry: Piccadilly Plaza, Manchester; 1962–65 by Covell, Matthew & Partners; 288 Transport: Bus Station and Car Park,
Preston; 1968–69 by Keith Ingham and Charles Wilson of Building Design Partnership

CONTENTS

BRUTALIST BRITAIN

This book describes some of the most forward-looking buildings ever seen in Britain, constructed on a scale and with an ambition unlikely to be repeated. We can wonder how they happened as we might admire an elephant or black rhinoceros; these buildings have a similar vulnerability. They are big, grizzled and – though 60 years is recent for a building – share a similar air of running out of time. Perhaps no other architecture is so distinctive and defines so short a period. The 1960s saw glitz and glamour, new products, young stardom and space-age science – real and fictional – like no other. Australians describe the fascination that these years hold, particularly for those too young to have been there, as 'the Austin Powers effect'. That so much sparkle was complemented by raw concrete may seem contradictory but, unlike expensive steel and inflexible brickwork, concrete could be pushed into almost any shape and size thanks to reinforcement and formwork.

Brutalism was the name widely if warily used to describe all that was biggest and boldest, even overweening, in modern architecture. It became a term of bemusement or even disgust, however, until the 2010s, when a new generation around the world rediscovered the buildings' power, sensuality and imagination, just at the point of their extinction. Few anywhere have statutory protection, but even the crudest have details that delight.

The opportunity to build on such an extensive scale came with the Second World War. The war saw 200,000 houses across Britain destroyed and 250,000 made uninhabitable, but equally important stimulants to renewal were backlogs of building from the 1930s, slum clearance, population growth

and migration. As early as January 1941 the popular magazine *Picture Post* devoted an issue to the rebuilding of Britain after the war. The editor Tom Hopkinson argued that 'Our plan for a new Britain is not something outside the war, or something after the war. It is an essential part of our war aims.'[1] His demands for decent food, education and healthcare saw expression in a government report on national insurance by William Beveridge published just as the war turned in Britain's favour late in 1942. Beveridge challenged five evils: want, idleness, ignorance, disease and squalor. Legislation for new schools and housing followed, and the Labour Government elected in 1945 introduced the National Health Service, nationalised and invested in heavy industry and transport, and initiated a programme of new towns.

Yet Britain was nearly bankrupted by the war, materials were in short supply and for the next decade the focus was on restoring industry and feeding the pent-up demand for goods. The greatest concern was that the mass unemployment of the inter-war years, hard-hitting in the North, Scotland and Wales, should not return. Economic recovery was delayed by the Suez Crisis of 1956; when it came, it unleashed the biggest construction programme Britain has ever seen, from schools and houses and new buildings for entertainment and sport to the remodelling of major city centres with offices, shops and car parks, and the building of whole new towns. The Conservative and Labour governments of the 1960s and early 1970s competed to have the largest building programmes. The Labour leader Harold Wilson argued for building in the 'white heat' of a scientific revolution based on new technology and cheap power, when speaking in Scarborough a year ahead of winning the general election of October 1964.

THE NEW BRUTALISM

While the French architect Le Corbusier was the movement's poster-boy, the term *brutalism* was coined in the United Kingdom. In its origins, it did not mean big or brash – though when Reyner Banham was asked in 1963 to write his epic account, *The New Brutalism*, his students were beginning to think that way. He describes a movement that began in the early 1950s with the Independent Group (a splinter group of young artists connected with the Institute of Contemporary Arts) at Saturday gatherings at the French pub in Dean Street and Sunday coffee mornings in his own home. The origins of the name remain mysterious, with Banham repeating gossip from the photographer Eric de Maré that 'new brutalism' had been used by Hans Asplund in Sweden in 1950 to describe hard-nosed buildings that countered the decorative new humanism that had become its national style – what we now term 'mid-century modern'.[2]

Smithdon School, Hunstanton, Norfolk, 1950–53 by Alison and Peter Smithson.

The architects Alison and Peter Smithson came to prominence when in 1950, aged 21 and 26 respectively, they won a competition for a secondary school in Hunstanton, Norfolk. Opened in 1953, though not fully completed until the following year, the design was inspired by Mies van der Rohe and a Royal Academy course in neo-classicism; Rudolf Wittkower's *Architectural Principles in the Age of Humanism*, published in 1948, not only reinvigorated the study of proportions but made them relevant to the era of the welfare state. Hunstanton is a steel structure and, though its finishes and services within and without are exposed, it slightly predates their thoughts on brutalism; nevertheless, its acclaim gave them a public platform. Guy Oddie, Peter's student friend, claimed that 'new brutalism' was coined at a dinner party given in about 1952 by Alison and their landlord Theo Crosby, as a pun on Peter's student nickname of Brutus – a comment on his profile and hated by Alison.[3] Reporting 'errors of fact' by Banham, the Smithsons explained that '"New Brutalism" was a spontaneous invention by A. M. S. [Alison] as a word-play counter-ploy to the *Architectural Review*'s "New Empiricism" ... The "brutal" part was taken from an English newspaper cutting which gave a translation from a French paper of a Marseilles official's attack on the Unité in construction, which described the building as "brutal".'[4] The historian Alan Powers unearthed the article on Le Corbusier's newly completed block of flats in Marseilles, the Unité d'habitation, which gave credence to this story. 'Alison coined it on the john,' Peter grunted when interviewed in the 1990s.

It is thus possible to link brutalism to the French term *béton brut*, concrete that is not smoothed down after casting but is left showing the patterns, seams and fixings of its formwork. It shares the rawness sought by Jean Dubuffet and his Art Brut movement in the 1940s. The Smithsons' own interest in outsider art bore fruit in the exhibition *Parallel of Life and Art* at the ICA

Unité d'habitation, Marseilles,
1947–52 by Le Corbusier.

in 1953, where they assisted their friends and collaborators Nigel Henderson and Eduardo Paolozzi in selecting illustrations of beauty in unorthodox places.

Banham was right to think of the new brutalism's greater formalism as a counter-movement to the prevalent enthusiasm for gentle Scandinavian design. This expressed the soft Swedish social democracy that was a model for the British welfare programme of the late 1940s. The two camps polarised in the architect's department of the London County Council (LCC), best seen in two prestigious housing estates situated barely a mile apart. Alton East expressed Scandinavian ideals and its architects' social commitment in contrasting brick and colourful tiles, while Alton West used storey-high concrete panels and a greater openness of scale. The two groups were later termed 'herbivores' and 'carnivores' by Hugh Casson and others, inspired by Michael Frayn's article recalling the 1951 Festival of Britain.[5]

The Smithsons, whose later career in writing and teaching honed their skills in self-publicity, were the only architects to embrace the term 'new brutalism'.[6] However, the work of Bill Howell, Stirling and Gowan, Colin St John Wilson and their partners followed a similar programme. In December 1953 the Smithsons illustrated a house whose construction in concrete, brick and wood would have been left exposed inside and out, commenting that 'had this been built, it would have been the first example of the New Brutalism'. A single-page manifesto entitled 'The New Brutalism', produced with Theo Crosby for *Architectural Design* in January 1955, considered the honest construction of brick and timber buildings as well as concrete to be brutalist, with references to Japanese temple architecture, 'peasant dwelling forms' and Frank Lloyd Wright as well as the Unité.[7] Banham followed with an article in the *Architectural Review* later in the year. John Summerson, a critic from an older generation, thought Banham had 'tickled up' the movement, but admitted that 'once every thirty years, there is a big sneeze in architecture. A new movement is due, and Mr Banham perfectly well knows it.'[8]

The first clear example of the new brutalism was a modest house in Watford by the Smithsons for an engineer and his wife, Derek and Jean Sugden. It appears externally conventional save for its large sloping roof and 'L'-shaped windows, though internally the brickwork and concrete beams are exposed and its joinery left unpainted. This was in tune with the Smithsons' growing belief in an architecture of 'ordinariness', introduced in an essay in 1952–53 and later defined as creating neutral spaces for clients to personalise, or what they called 'inhabitation'. Their London offices for *The Economist* magazine built in 1962–64 were a neat reinterpretation of classical proportions clad in stone. In their later schemes – including housing at Robin Hood Gardens – it was the planning and above all the routes through a building or complex that became critical.

FOREIGN INFLUENCES

British architects quickly made the pilgrimage to Marseilles to see Le Corbusier's Unité d'habitation. It was a special commission, built with government support to honour the Marseillais' bitter fight against Hitler, and was the climax of Le Corbusier's long career planning decent flats at extremely high densities. As *The Times* reported, 'The building has from the first provoked violent controversy, and a campaign was recently launched against the architect for erecting a building which "presents drawbacks of a moral character, contrary to French style and aesthetic standards".' Opposition to brutalism began early. The Unité is a giant slab some 17 storeys high and three times as long, though counting the storeys is difficult since many spaces are of double height, including the open ground floor where the building's weight is borne on two lines of pilotis or piers resembling the flippers of a troupe of giant seals. The block originally stood in open land and even today has few amenities nearby, so two of its upper floors are lined with shops, a café and professional chambers (for doctors, solicitors etc.), while the rooftop featured a crèche and running track. The in-situ concrete bore the marks of its timber shuttering and precast parts were rubbed down to expose a rough aggregate. The juxtaposition of different proportional systems, mixed uses, complex sections, heavy materials and pilotis became the basic language for brutalism in its heroic form of a decade later.

Architects did not have to visit Le Corbusier's buildings to experience their thrall. Born Charles-Édouard Jeanneret, the architect first came to prominence as a journalist, adopting a pseudonym based on an old family name and playing on its imagery of a 'corbeau' or raven. He then became the first modern architect to publish all his buildings and projects. Eight volumes of the *Oeuvre Complète* appeared between 1929 and 1970, with summaries in English and German, in which he addressed the problems of high-density urban living, traffic planning and modern housing ahead of anyone else. Their publication was a major event. Alison Smithson admitted that 'When you open a new volume of the *Oeuvre Complète* you find that he has had all your best ideas already, has done what you were about to do next.'[9] Before the war he had produced a series of elegant, white-walled concrete houses, then used the same wholly modern idiom while reconnecting with traditional stonework. But after the war his work embraced rugged textures and complex proportions. As well as five unités, including one in Berlin, Le Corbusier designed two seminal religious buildings – the chapel of Notre Dame du Haut at Ronchamp (1954) and the monastery of La Tourette at Éveux near Lyons (1960), and a capitol complex for the new city of Chandigarh in India (1954–64).

The generation of architects born in the 1920s and early 1930s took information from an increasing number of foreign sources. With more books and magazines available, and greater opportunities to travel – particularly on student scholarships – it became easier for young architects to look still further afield for inspiration.

Assembly Building with Secretariat to rear, Chandigarh, 1954–64 by Le Corbusier.

James Morris and Robert Steedman secured Carnegie scholarships to explore Europe on a motorbike in 1953, when the Unité at Marseilles was one of the few new buildings to have been completed. Then, in 1956, they won scholarships to study in Philadelphia, where their lecturers included Ian McHarg, Philip Johnson and Louis Kahn.

When Peter Womersley first began working in Scotland in the mid-1950s, his private houses had closely followed Miesian lines. But then, as he explained in 1969, 'How long can you develop an intellectual ideal, particularly if it has to get more "less" all the time? Should not every building be a fresh re-building of experience gained on other buildings? Should there not be development and enrichment at all times, if atrophy is not to set in?'[10] While his contemporary Robert Venturi wrote that 'less is a bore' and developed post-modernism, Womersley found what he called 'heart' from brutalism. The buildings he listed as exemplars were admired by many of his contemporaries. They began with Frank Lloyd Wright's Fallingwater and Le Corbusier's Pavillon Suisse and Ronchamp chapel, then moved on to buildings by the next generation, including Kenzo Tange's Olympic buildings and Kunio Maekawa's concert halls in Tokyo, John Andrews's Scarborough College near Toronto, the Marchiondi Institute by Vittoriano Viganò at Milan, and Skidmore Owings & Merrill's Mauna Kea Hotel on Hawaii.

In 1955, James Stirling was one of the first British architects to visit Le Corbusier's Maisons Jaoul, a pair of new houses in Neuilly-sur-Seine on the edge of Paris. Their board-marked concrete frames and arched vaults, along with a crude infill of rough brickwork, were inspired by the vernacular of northern India seen by Le Corbusier at Chandigarh. In turn the idiom can be found in housing and university buildings around Britain as perhaps nowhere else. For Banham the greater emotionalism of Stirling's

Engineering Building, University of Leicester, 1959–63 by Stirling and Gowan.

work with James Gowan made it more exciting than the Smithsons' restrained Economist group (1962–64) and heralded the dynamic 1960s after years of austerity. 'I suppose they'll call it brutalism,' Stirling grumbled in 1961, anticipating reaction to his and Gowan's re-interpretation of a Victorian working-class terrace at Avenham, Preston (demolished).[11] Their engineering faculty building for the University of Leicester was Britain's most distinctive post-war building, the red brickwork and north rooflights of local factories combined with the exaggerated angles of Russian constructivism. Stirling (without Gowan) went on to design still more controversial buildings at Cambridge and Oxford, which together have become known as the Red Trilogy.

Another version of the Maisons Jaoul, on a far grander scale, was Churchill College, Cambridge, built to train the budding scientists of the space age. The competition held in 1959 marked a coming-of-age for modernism; after a decade where it had become the natural vehicle for lightweight schools and housing, the competition brief asked for a design of our times that would last 500 years and be a memorial to Britain's wartime hero. Stirling and Gowan's design was shortlisted, but the winners were Richard Sheppard, Robson & Partners, who devised a concrete frame infilled with gnarled yellow brick and made a feature of giant arched vaults over Cambridge's largest dining hall.

RAW CONCRETE

The Second World War had seen building materials in short supply, and concrete was used for huts, hangars and housing. These shortages continued into the 1950s, in part because brickmaking could not keep up with demand, in part because of the pound's poor exchange rate against the dollar, which limited the amount of softwood and steel that could be imported from Scandinavia. A wartime licensing system remained in force until November 1954 to direct materials into essential housing, schools and industry. Brick shortages continued through the 1950s, and a crisis when the economy boomed in 1960–62 was exacerbated in early 1963 by three months of snow and frost across Britain. The LCC resorted to erecting prefabricated bungalows, not seen since the mid-1940s, and authorities everywhere explored new construction methods that were quick, economical and required little skilled manpower (also in desperately short supply).

Concrete again provided the solution. The Romans had exploited the hydraulic lime and pozzolanic ash binders that occur naturally in southern Italy to build structures ranging from harbour walls to the Pantheon. In Britain, cement (lime mixed with ash or brick dust) was being produced artificially in commercial quantities by the early 19th century, and became a fashionable alternative to stone for facing middle-class terraced housing. Mixed with aggregate it formed a quick-setting concrete for harbour walls and workers' cottages. Inserting iron reinforcements followed in the 1850s, making possible concrete columns and beams. It was in France where the most significant inventions were made and above all marketed, led by François Hennebique, a building contractor turned engineer who disseminated his efficient reinforcement system through a series of approved contractors across Europe and beyond. In 1895 he dispatched a senior engineer, Louis Gustave Mouchel, to erect a granary and flour mill in Swansea and to establish a London office.

The first concrete structures concealed their raw guts behind brick or stone façades, partly for good manners and partly because of building regulations. It took until the mid-1920s, with buildings such as London's Fortune Theatre and the Wembley Exhibition, for concrete to be recognised as beautiful in Britain. In the 1930s it became a statement of forward thinking and efficiency, as at Marlborough College, Wiltshire, where the memorial assembly hall is classical and the science laboratories of exposed concrete, yet designed by the same architect, W. G. Newton. This trend became still more important in the 1950s and 1960s, encompassing almost every building type.

While new techniques permitted larger schools, taller flats and more complex factories, they could also look more interesting. Sand or pebble aggregates offered infinite variations in colours and textures, sparkling where a sliver of mica or a grainy texture caught the low British sunlight. White concrete showed a careful choice of materials, since cement naturally darkens over time. Rich board-marking was a sign of sophistication; at the National Theatre the formwork was of carefully chosen Douglas fir, each piece to be used only twice since slurry would lodge and blur the pattern of its graining. Textures could be further enhanced by brushing or hammering the concrete as it cured: large aggregate could be exposed, or a cast ribbed finish partly chipped away – effective at London Zoo's Elephant House and South Norwood Library.

Concrete's elemental quality suited it for churches, theatres and art galleries, offering more than an ability to bridge large spans without intervening columns. It made possible the more open, wider structures that followed new thinking in both churches and theatres that sought to throw clergy and congregations, actors and audiences, closer together. It also provided a framework for stained glass and works of art. Indeed, concrete was also a medium for art itself. When in 1957 William Mitchell and Anthony Hollaway were employed by the London County Council as its first artists, they had to work with materials that cost no more than those being used for the buildings they were decorating. Their media thus became the concrete and bricks found on site, moulded or blasted in any way possible, plus what they termed 'rubbish' such as broken tiles and glass.

NEW TECHNIQUES

Reinforced concrete became steadily more sophisticated. Building regulations for new materials were most rigorous in London, so the greatest innovation was generally found elsewhere in Britain. Concrete's tensile qualities were increased with the pre-stressing or post-tensioning of steel wires through the concrete, patented in France by Eugène Freyssinet in 1929 and proven when in 1934 he rescued Le Havre's subsiding maritime railway station. Wires were run through the mould before the concrete was poured. They could be pre-tensioned, though most were post-tensioned after the concrete had partly cured. Pre-stressing had barely reached Britain by the war but was quickly adopted in the early 1950s for large spans following its success in a bus garage at Bournemouth. As important were the arrival of 300ft (91m) high tower cranes such as Big Alphonse, imported from France by the contractors Wates for building tall flats, mainly for the LCC. Smaller cranes ran on

rails, making it essential that blocks be planned in straight lines at system-built estates such as Morris Walk (demolished), Broadwater Farm and Aylesbury.

The war saw advances in pre-casting, a simpler way of producing slabs and beams than pouring concrete into timber formwork erected in situ. Factories offered better working conditions and enabled the concrete to be finished to the highest standard, as with the storey-high panels of Alton West. The results can be more beautiful than stone, since they are so precisely controlled, but are almost impossible to replicate once a building is completed. The Cement and Concrete Association opened a research centre at Wexham Springs in 1947, building a series of offices and laboratories in a landscape with fencing and sculptures to demonstrate different methods of concrete construction and finishes, adding a training college at Fulmer Grange next door in 1966. Today, the only survivor on the redeveloped site is William Mitchell's primeval sculpture *Corn King and Spring Queen*, from 1964.

The forgotten boom of the 1950s was in building power stations, bringing yet more contracts to the major construction companies and seemingly infinite supplies of cheap energy with the completion of the national grid across the United Kingdom. Electricity remained cheap until the early 1970s, when coal miners' strikes and a 300 per cent rise in oil prices brought a dramatic end to a luxury that had been taken for granted. Many council homes suddenly became too expensive to heat. Reliable electricity meant that a sealed and air-conditioned environment became possible, and houses, shops and offices could have large open plans. These could be brilliantly lit for the first time, for at last artificial lighting became reliable; cold cathode and fluorescent fittings appeared in the war and were first adopted for civilian use in the public hall over Peckham's Co-operative store in July 1949.

Structures became larger as more functions, boiler plants and covered parking were added.

The architect Owen Luder explained in 2009 that 'because you couldn't get steel, you used in-situ concrete as it was the only thing you could do. That meant that the big contractors were doing the foundations and building frame, then they brought in specialist sub-contractors to do the rest. This was also the beginning of prefabrication off-site, bringing things in on a separate package. The concrete was exposed because it was the structure, and you can use the shutter boarding as a finish in various ways. Contractors didn't realise how expensive concrete was to do, and for a time it was under-priced – by the late 1960s they realised, and it became expensive.'[12]

Luder was referring to the large construction companies that came to the fore during the Second World War and expanded further thereafter, winning large contracts in the new towns and in town centres. When after 1953 central government subsidies for public housing focused on slum clearance, with extra grants for building tall flats, these contractors began to license building systems from France, Denmark and Sweden, where prefabricated solutions to the chronic housing shortages had already been developed. They built their own factories to cast the concrete panels and beams. By the late 1960s seven companies dominated the housing market: George Wimpey, Britain's largest contractor; John Laing & Son and Taylor Woodrow, their closest competitors; Concrete Ltd, the largest materials firm and licensees of the Bison system developed in Dartford, Kent; Wates, housing specialists with their own methodology; Camus (Great Britain), a subsidiary of the French giants who entered the British market via Liverpool in 1963; and Crudens Ltd, a Scottish company that held the licence to the Swedish Skarne system. By the late 1960s, Laing alone were employing over 10,000 men. Many firms had connections to the Conservative Party – Keith Joseph was heir to the Bovis company and Geoffrey Rippon a director of Cubitts – but it was the Labour Government of 1964 that made

a condition of financing public housing that it should be system-built. George Finch, working for the LCC and the London Borough of Lambeth, recalled that 'you had to develop strong arguments not to use a system. Local authorities were being strongly pushed and housing committees found it hard to resist the pressure.'[13]

THINKING BIG

Summerson's 'big sneeze' saw the younger generation blow apart the international debating shop on modernism, the Congrès Internationaux d'Architecture Moderne founded in 1928. After organising its tenth meeting at Dubrovnik in 1956, a group of younger architects including the Smithsons formed a breakaway organisation appropriately called Team 10. Early studies for Dubrovnik on the theme of 'Habitat' produced by the English contingent (the Smithsons, Stirling, Bill Howell, John Partridge, Colin St John Wilson, Peter Carter and John Voelcker) had rejected freestanding tower blocks for lower-rise schemes that huggled round new street patterns. They suggested possibilities for public housing that began to appear for real in inner London a decade later. Once central heating and motor cars became affordable for council tenants around 1960, it made sense to stretch long slabs over basement parking, creating enclosed precincts in place of the traditional street pattern. Team 10 members encouraged an international style of large units that covered a variety of functions within city centres, new towns or universities like a giant overcoat. These they called 'mat building', but a more common term by the 1970s was the 'megastructure', derived from the artificial planets of science fiction such as Larry Niven's *Ringworld* of 1970.

While many architects turned to teaching and exhibition work to support themselves between building projects, in the Smithsons' case for many years, a few made a permanent career in this growing world of pure ideas. They were liberated by not having to make their projects remotely buildable, as can be seen in the largely theoretical work of Cedric Price and particularly of the six architects associated with *Archigram* magazine, whose most sought-after issues adopted the look of science-fiction comics. Telegrams may be no more, but the word amalgamated with 'architecture' still has a buzz to it. Peter Cook, David Greene and Michael Webb came straight from college, but Warren Chalk and Ron Herron had earlier worked for the LCC, moving from schools to detail the South Bank centre where they were joined by Dennis Crompton and in 1961 met Theo Crosby, who found them work with the builders Taylor Woodrow to support their reveries. Here the ambitions of the 1960s could assume boundless possibilities, but in turn inspire what might actually be buildable. An exhibition at the ICA, *Walking City*, led by Herron, envisioned London remodelled with giant beetle-like structures, while Cook's *Plug-In City* saw buildings as adjuncts to a network of roads and services, repurposing an old city for constant change. He and Greene reimagined the design as a shopping centre for the latter's native Nottingham, though in fact the group's only buildings before the 1980s were a playground in Milton Keynes and a swimming pool for the singer Rod Stewart.

Here was a background for what might have happened if more money and materials had been available. We might scoff at the idea of two motorways coursing through Brixton, south London, but Magda Borowiecka's barrier block and George Finch's recreation centre raised on a pedestrian walkway remind us that until 1972 these roads were expected to happen. Only the City of London had the means and political stability to see a project to its end; hence the importance of the Barbican, first planned by Chamberlin, Powell & Bon in 1955 and built between 1963 and 1982 with little wavering of purpose and no short cuts.

REBUILDING CITY CENTRES

What happened elsewhere was generally more prosaic. Lord Reith had encouraged bombed-out cities to plan 'boldly and imaginatively' for the future, using the same words wherever he went. This wartime 'can do' continued through the 1960s. Changes to towns and cities were inevitable, not least where the war had left empty craters or blackened carcases that were crumbling away after 15 years without maintenance. These were, however, only a catalyst for more development in areas already declared 'blighted' by overcrowding and a lack of sanitation. Their redevelopment was made easier by systems of compulsory purchase and compensation introduced in the Town and Country Planning Act of 1947. The same Act also introduced a tax on the profits of development (known as betterment), stalling private building, though it did not stop speculators from acquiring land cheaply ahead of the day in 1952 when a new Conservative Government repealed that part of the legislation. A new breed of estate agent-turned-developer then got rich erecting shops and offices, financed by compensation from the War Damage Commission and investment from insurance companies or pension funds. Among the first were Louis Freedman and Fred Maynard of Ravenseft, who built in the most badly bombed cities such as Bristol and Hull. They were followed by Jack Cotton, Charles Clore and Harold Samuel, who catered for the growing demand for offices, particularly in London.

Two great cultural changes were apparent in Britain by the late 1950s, having already transformed the United States. One was the growth of the shopping precinct and department store to serve a more affluent population, the other the mass ownership of motor cars. In 1959 Malcolm MacEwen reported that vehicle registrations in Britain had risen by 8.2 per cent since 1946 and mileage almost as much; cars had doubled in number in nine years and would triple in 13 more.[11] A product of this prosperity

Former Unicorn Hotel and car park, Bristol, 1963–66 by Wakeford, Jerram & Harris.

was the rise in traffic accidents. There were 5,526 fatalities in 1956 alone, half of them pedestrians.[15] An early solution was Colin St John Wilson and Peter Carter's concept of the 'vertical-city' for the CIAM meeting in Dubrovnik, featuring a high-level pedestrian podium, office towers and a helicopter. The theme of movement through a city, with pedestrians separated from fast-moving cars, reappeared in many entries to an international competition in 1958 to reunite central 'Hauptstadt' Berlin. The Smithsons won third place with a series of giant platforms across Friedrichstrasse and the surrounding neighbourhood, setting shops and parking below them, cafés and entertainment facilities on the new level and offices above. A similar scheme was that by Percy Johnson-Marshall, one of the first planners to work for the LCC on the South Bank, with Colin Buchanan, author in 1963 of a crucial government report, *Traffic in Towns*. Several of these schemes, with their futuristic images, were collected in 1960 by Theo Crosby in the journal *Uppercase 3*, an early showcase for space-age design contemporary with the first Roneo-printed *Archigram*.

Reinforced concrete was essential for the larger shops and offices that began to appear in town centres, and especially for multi-storey car parks. Small car parks had been built before 1945 as enclosed buildings mainly to serve theatregoers, but large, open-sided structures with exposed rooftop parking proved the cheapest and most popular option, becoming standard once the LCC eased its restrictions in 1960. In Sheffield and Portsmouth, retail and wholesale markets were built on several levels with service roads and parking, requiring structures that could support heavy and differential loads. For simpler car parks, concrete could be cast as well as poured in situ, including the Texan 'lift-slab' system whereby floor slabs were cast on the ground and then raised by hydraulic jacks. More sophisticated car parks were built as a continuous poured ramp to ease circulation. Specialist companies such as Parcar and Multidek made patterns of their semi-open façades of pre-cast panels, notably at the Unicorn Hotel (1963–66) next to Bristol's Floating Harbour, which has its own car park alongside, and at Welbeck Street, London (1968–70, demolished). The patterns were christened 'Double Diamonds' after a popular beer of the time.

As more young people were attracted to London's bright lights and better jobs, so more remote areas faced decline. An extreme example was mid-Wales, where the 1961 census showed a decline of 17 per cent over a decade when Britain's population had risen by 5.3 per cent. In Powys the medieval Newtown, whose population had fallen by a fifth, was declared a government new town in 1967 to encourage investment in jobs and housing. The most obvious result was a new office block, the brick-faced Ladywell House, built in 1973–74 to attract a broader range of employment.

Other local authorities redeveloped their town centres without such government help. Since they faced restrictions on the rates they could levy on industrial premises, they sought to raise income by investing in the valuable sites of former wholesale markets and abattoirs. They also wanted a modern image for their town with new jobs to keep young people there. In 1958 the depressed Tyneside town of Jarrow, ill-famed for its hunger marches in the 1930s, appointed Arnold Hagenbach and Sam Chippindale of Arndale Properties to revive its town centre with a smart new shopping precinct. Arndale followed this with a market square in Shipley, West Yorkshire. Soon every town was in competition for the tallest flats, shiniest shops and latest in entertainment. London's Elephant and Castle and Birmingham's Bullring, both built in 1960–64 and now demolished, were the first indoor shopping centres to be built in Britain, but Arndale became their greatest exponents after Chippindale visited the United States and Australia. Local authorities provided the land, and Arndale supplied the design and management in return for a very favourable rent, with architectural detailing secondary to layouts and services.

The city of Newcastle upon Tyne wanted something more. Labour had taken control in 1958, and its leader from 1960 was T. Dan Smith, a silky-tongued operator who saw rebuilding the city centre as key to broadening the local economy and keeping hold of the population. He claimed that the council was moribund and stuffed with reactionaries; to find a planning officer, he flew around Britain in a chartered plane to interview likely candidates before selecting Wilfred Burns, previously of Surrey and Coventry councils. Burns inherited an existing scheme for new roads across the River Tyne, and promoted more across the city centre – arguing that a good road junction was 'an exciting new element to be added as a positive feature to the central area landscape'.[16] Smith talked of a 'space age Newcastle' and a 'new Brasilia', promising 'revolution rather than evolution'.[17] His schemes included a new central shopping area and a university for 20,000 students. Sir Basil Spence, already working at the university, designed a central library and shopping precinct, an extension to the Laing

The Tricorn Centre, Portsmouth, 1964–66 by Owen Luder Partnership (demolished).

Art Gallery and flats, and supplied elevations to an office development by Ravenseft. A more dramatic intervention was Swan House, a seven-storey office block built in 1963–69 by Robert Matthew, Johnson-Marshall & Partners on Burns's most prominent traffic island. Smith's coup would have been a 28-storey hotel in Eldon Square by Arne Jacobsen, who in 1967 opened a Newcastle office; finance was sought from Forte Holdings, but its merger with Trust Houses brought delays and rising inflation ended the scheme.[18] Eldon Square was rebuilt in the 1970s as a bland shopping centre, amid objections from a growing conservation lobby.

Meanwhile, on the south bank of the River Tyne, Gateshead had already determined to rebuild its own run-down high street. Developers were invited to give the town 'a new heart', and in April 1961 a scheme by Millerdale Properties, a local consortium backed by the developer E. Alec Colman and the electricity industry's superannuation funds, was selected.[19] The London architect Owen Luder produced a layout in ten days, to which his partner Rodney Gordon added the elevations, with the detailed drawings done locally. Completed in 1969, the

Trinity Centre formed a pedestrian oasis amid a new freeway system serving the Tyne bridges, an open square behind high-street shops from which escalators ascended to a market and a further square on the higher level of West Street behind. A multi-storey car park was crucial in that location and grew as the scheme evolved. The film director Mike Hodges was a friend of Gordon's, so used the site while it was under construction for his film *Get Carter*. After decades of neglect, the building was demolished in 2010 to make way for a conventional Tesco superstore.

A similar story followed at Portsmouth, always a penurious city with a low rates income. Here Colman secured a site identified for a wholesale market and again added shops and parking. Building to Luder and Gordon's designs started in April 1964 and the Tricorn Centre

Elephant and Castle Shopping Centre, 1960–64 by Boissevain & Osmond (demolished).

opened in 1966. Luder described how 'the car park and wholesale market were reached via a ramp at each end done in situ. Corbusian details crept in when I wasn't looking, with very interesting window details. The earliest schemes didn't have the sculptural forms. How we made a design three-dimensional and interesting is important. The overhead service road for the shops and market at Portsmouth was also important. You had to get lorries up the ramps, and they became sculptural circular ramps – they really became quite a feature. The size of the service lorries would be an issue in the continued use of the building – in the 1960s they were smaller than now. Below the market was a pedestrian precinct, with sculptural treatments for the pedestrian stairs from the car park and a sculptural quality to the whole. In the later 1960s the contractors priced up this work and it became too expensive to do. Tricorn was not as successful as it should have been. But the nightclub had the big pop stars and was popular with students. We did out one pub and the brewery did the other – the Bell. The developer could have signed up the shops in 1963 but he decided to wait until completion and cash in. But in 1965 the commercial market collapsed, and he didn't get the key tenants and he moved the supermarket from the back to the front.'[20] The shops failed – without an anchor store, they were simply too far from the main Commercial Road – and the Tricorn Centre was demolished in 2004. The land is still empty nearly 20 years later.

Here, rather than in the Smithsons' theories, lay the essence of brutalism. Good looks had to fit the commercial budget, and Luder's design partner Rodney Gordon found that adding projecting bays and stairs to the exterior helped achieve larger office spaces. Similarly, Ian Nairn noted how a new development in Manchester's Piccadilly Gardens by Covell, Matthews & Partners, featuring a hotel and offices set over a podium with a car park and shopping arcade, evolved between its first designs in 1961 and

Swan House, Newcastle upon Tyne, 1963–69 by Robert Matthew, Johnson-Marshall & Partners.

completion in 1965. Ian Nairn remarked how 'the way in which all of the parts of the Piccadilly Hotel have grown knobs ... is a potted history of recent architectural fashion'.[21] Here can still be seen many of the elements of 'high brutalism' at its best – a large mixed-use scheme that erased the old street plan with a raised walkway over a bus stand and car parking, its elevations with board-marked concrete, William Mitchell decoration and chunky plastic signage, a projecting conference theatre and servicing and (now gone) a wavy roof. There is a spiral car ramp, and the pedestrian walkway was planned to continue along Portland Street with premises for the Bank of England by Fitzroy Robinson & Partners, one of three regional branches developed with Trafalgar House.

More 'serious' architects working for the universities also introduced bays and projections. This was often in a genuine scientific attempt to throw off rainwater and prevent it from running down windows and then staining the concrete below, as well as for their romantic possibilities. One protagonist was the multi-disciplinary

practice of Arup Associates, where the principal architect in the 1960s was Philip Dowson, who detailed the Minerals and Physical Metallurgy Building at Birmingham University of 1963–66 with concealed gutters within the concrete frame, and later set his large windows behind the concrete structure so it formed a frame to views looking out. The other was Howell, Killick, Partridge and Amis, who set their windows forward in pre-cast modules that resembled the squares in a bar of chocolate, first seen at the Ashley and Strathcona Buildings at Birmingham University in 1961–62 and additions to St Anne's College, Oxford, made in 1964–67.

THE DECLINE OF BRUTALISM

Describing Manchester in 1960, Ian Nairn lamented how 'urban renewal ... so often means replacing lively old dirt by dead new cleanness'.[22] Even the most powerful brutalism only served to reinforce the views of a growing movement, beginning with Jane Jacobs's *Death* and *Life of Great American Cities*, that urban areas should have a dense mix of different buildings and real streets to walk in.[23] A decade later, a short building boom coincided with rampant inflation, leading to lower finishes and the curtailment of projects like the Brunswick Centre in London. Edward Heath's Conservative Government (1970–74) sought to stem the conflicting problems of rising inflation and rising unemployment by investing in more public works and lifting Labour's controls on bank lending and office building; three times as much capital went into property development as into industrial production. Insurance and pension fund investment in property was estimated at £4,000 million by 1974, ensuring that profit was the critical factor in any scheme and there was little money for a decent design.[24]

Still more wretched was corruption, as unscrupulous architects and developers tapped up humble working-class councillors in small authorities not used to dealing with large building contracts. John G. L. Poulson was the most notorious of these architects and T. Dan Smith the council leader who fell furthest, having made deals with a particularly ineffective house-building system, though perhaps the greatest casualty was Reginald Maudling, Heath's home secretary. Local authority architects were also convicted of corruption, among them the Bradford city architect W. Clifford Brown and Birmingham's Alan Maudsley, who was sentenced to six years after living what his obituarist called 'a high life of golf, gambling, girls and world travel'.[25]

As schemes grew larger, so modern architecture began to be discredited. Large clearance schemes were blamed for a loss of community and identity; instead, a combination of gentrification and squatting showed that the old inner cities could have a new life. The biggest blow was the collapse of a block of flats in Canning Town, Ronan Point, erected using the Larsen-Nielsen system from Denmark, using large prefabricated panels that were self-supporting. These were fine in low- or medium-rise estates such as the LCC's Morris Walk, Woolwich, but the London Borough of Newham pushed the system to 23 storeys, almost double the height of previous Larsen-Nielsen schemes. Early on 16 May 1968, a badly connected gas cooker exploded, blowing out a load-bearing wall and causing the living rooms down one corner of the building to collapse; the death toll was limited to five only because most people were still asleep. An inquiry blamed an over-reliance on load-bearing joints and poor workmanship, while new housing snuggled into a neo-vernacular dress or applied post-modern details.[26]

THE BRUTALIST REVIVAL

Nikolaus Pevsner, who had supervised Banham's PhD, gave a talk on the BBC's Third Programme in December 1966, which was published in *The Listener* magazine. In it he set out his reservations about expressionism in architecture and brutalism in particular. No deliberate publicity campaign could have been more successful, and more articles followed in the national press, including a review of *The New Brutalism* by Pevsner in *The Guardian*. While generous about the book, he was unequivocal about his distaste for the Leicester Engineering Building or Churchill College, Cambridge. Thereafter, the term never quite went away, sultry yet tempting, or like a deliberately difficult novel for sixth-formers.

The first stab at post-war listing came in 1987, and with only buildings over 30 years old eligible for consideration brutalism could be safely ignored. A spate of listing cases then followed in 1989–90, including Alexander Fleming House, the Barbican, and the Queen Elizabeth Hall and Hayward Gallery complex on London's South Bank, none successful but forcing English Heritage to take a stand. In 1992 the Thirties Society became the Twentieth Century

Society to better defend post-war heritage. More cases followed, notably Preston Bus Station in 1998 and Birmingham Central Library in 2004. In 2012 the Twentieth Century Society placed these structures and the South Bank complex on the World Monuments Watch. No other cases were as important at the time. Birmingham Library was demolished but the others have been restored, and Preston Bus Station was listed in 2013 thanks to the tenacity of the society's caseworker and local campaigners.

Brutalism, meanwhile, became fashionable, as the growing internet allowed more younger and less-established historians to declare their reaction to the tame neo-modernism of the 1990s. After producing his first blogs in 2005, Owen Hatherley published a series of laments for a lost if lavender-tinted 1960s, *Militant Modernism* and *A Guide to the New Ruins of Great Britain*, in 2009 and 2010 respectively. John Grindrod in 2013 similarly explored what had happened to post-war Britain, rechristened *Concretopia*, starting in his native Croydon. A book by Alexander Clement, *Brutalism*, claimed an array of buildings as brutalist – including Centre Point, a building inspired by Oscar Niemeyer that made an interplay of sunlight and movement. It saw the start of an alarming movement to claim every modern building for brutalism, but nevertheless marked a moment in time before many major buildings disappeared.

By the time that Barnabas Calder's passionate yet informed *Raw Concrete: The Beauty of Brutalism* was published in 2016, there were brutalist map guides, brutalist postcards, plates, mugs and even tea towels.[27] Brutalism was photogenic, and art books followed from the most obscure corners of the world. Boston and other North American cities formed their own conservation campaigns, leading in 2012 to a conference in Berlin and in 2017 to an exhibition in Frankfurt, *SOS Brutalism – Save the Concrete Monsters*, and an accompanying book that surveyed buildings from around the world.[28]

In Portsmouth, the local radio had called for the demolition of the Tricorn Centre, encouraging its listeners to call English Heritage with their views. It duly came down in 2004. But then a series of blogs and books captured a wave of nostalgia for its shops, pubs and nightclub. It was a reminder of another tenet held by Jacobs, reflected in her title *Death and Life*, that city centres need cheap, adaptable spaces for new businesses and arts activities to start and grow, and in its last years the Tricorn Centre demonstrated this perfectly – a mantle now assumed by Anglia Square in the heart of genteel Norwich. Campaigners for the Tricorn lost their building but subsequently won the debate as books, blogs and nostalgia took over, while it is only in 2022 that there are firm proposals for the site. Brutalism's greatest publicity came in 2014 with a two-part series on BBC television by Jonathan Meades, *Bunkers, Brutalism and Bloodymindedness*. It may have said more about Meades than the buildings but, as he declared, 'You don't go knocking down Stonehenge or Lincoln Cathedral. I think buildings like the Tricorn were as good as that. They were great monuments of an age.'[29] Campaigns like that for Anglia Square in 2022 show that the buildings still have a relevance today.

A NOTE ON LISTING

Buildings over 30 years old from the start of their construction can generally be considered for listing; younger buildings have to be under threat and of outstanding interest to be considered, particularly in England. England and Wales have a system of grade I and II* for buildings of outstanding interest and grade II for those of special interest (about 90 per cent of listings across all time periods). Scotland has a separate system of grade A for outstanding interest, B for special interest and C or C+ for buildings which contribute to a group or which are ancillary to other listings.

FOOTNOTES

1 Tom Hopkinson, *Picture Post*, vol.10, no.1, 4 January 1941, p.4.

2 *Architectural Review*, vol.120, no.715, August 1956, p.72; Reyner Banham, *The New Brutalism*, London, Architectural Press, 1966, p.10.

3 Guy Oddie in conversation, 24 February 2006.

4 'Banham's Bumper Book on Brutalism, Discussed by Alison and Peter Smithson', *Architects' Journal*, vol.144, no.26, 28 December 1966, p.1590; '"Radiant City Lawsuit", Complaint of Brutal Realism', *The Times*, No.52486, 4 December 1952, p.6.

5 Michael Frayn, 'Festival', in Michael Sissons and Philip French eds., *Age of Austerity*, London, Hodder and Stoughton, 1963, p.336.

6 'House in Soho', *Architectural Design*, vol.23, no.12, December 1953, p.342.

7 'The New Brutalism', *Architectural Design*, vol.25, no.1, January 1955, p.1.

8 'New Brutalism Defined at Last', *Architects' Journal*, 12 April 1956, p.339.

9 Reyner Banham, 'The Last Formgiver', *Architectural Review*, vol.140, no.834, August 1966, pp.97–108.

10 Peter Womersley, 'Architects' Approach to Architecture', *RIBA Journal*, May 1969, p.192.

11 *RAIC Journal* (Architecture Canada), vol.45, no.4, April 1968, p.44.

12 Owen Luder in conversation, Gateshead, 24 June 2009.

13 George Finch in conversation, 13 January 2006.

14 Malcolm MacEwen, 'Motropolis', *Architects' Journal*, vol.130, no.3363, 1 October 1959, pp.254–63.

15 C. D. Buchanan, *Mixed Blessing: The Motor in Britain*, London, Leonard Hill, 1958, p.83.

16 Wilfred Burns, *Newcastle, a Study in Replanning at Newcastle upon Tyne*, London, Leonard Hill, 1967, p.25.

17 'Space for everyone in the wonderful new Newcastle', *Evening Chronicle*, no.26123, 12 April 1961, p.8.

18 *City News*, September 1969, p.3, in Newcastle City Archives N536(B), with thanks to Grace McCombie.

19 *Gateshead Post*, no.703, 28 April 1961, p.1; 'Putting a New Heart into an Old Town', *The Journal*, no.37340, 16 June 1966, p.10.

20 Owen Luder in conversation, Gateshead, 24 June 2009.

21 'High Piccadilly', *Architect and Building News*, vol.215, no.17, 29 April 1959, p.549; vol.227, no.46, 17 November 1965, pp.913–16; Ian Nairn, 'Patrician Manchester', *The Listener*, vol.64, no.1644, 29 September 1960, pp.505–7; Nairn, *Britain's Changing Towns*, BBC, 1967, p.45.

22 Ian Nairn, 'Patrician Manchester', *The Listener*, vol.64, no.1644, 29 September 1960, pp.505–7.

23 Jane Jacobs, *The Death and Life of Great American Cities*, New York, Random House, 1961.

24 Malcolm MacEwen, *Crisis in Architecture*, London, RIBA, 1974, p.27.

25 https://www.thefreelibrary.com/ Disgraced+ architect+dies%2C+aged+84%3B+OBITUARY. -a060531893, accessed 14 February 2022.

26 MHLG, *Report of the Inquiry into the Collapse of Flats at Ronan Point*, Canning Town, London, HMSO, 1968, pp.5–17.

27 Barnabas Calder, *Raw Concrete: The Beauty of Brutalism*, London, William Heinemann, 2016.

28 Oliver Elser, Philip Kurz, Peter Cachola Schmal, eds., *SOS Brutalism*, Zurich, Park Books, 2017.

29 Quoted in James Kidd, 'Death, Brutalism and pre-pubertal sex: Jonathan Meades embraces some difficult subjects in his TV series and memoir', *The Independent*, 22 February 2014, https://www.independent.co.uk/ news/people/profiles/death-brutalism-and- prepubertal-sex-jonathan-meades-embraces- some-difficult-subjects-in-his-tv-series-and- memoir-9144497.html, accessed 15 February 2022.

PRIVATE HOUSES AND FLATS

LANGHAM HOUSE CLOSE

Ham Common, Richmond, London
1957–58; James Stirling and James Gowan
Listed grade II*

In 1955 James Stirling secured a commission for a series of flats on a tight site tucked behind an 18th-century house facing Ham Common. He produced a three-storey block based on Le Corbusier's Maisons Jaoul, which he was the first British architect to visit on its completion in 1956. His review of the houses for the *Architectural Review* established the mix of brick and concrete, 'L'-shaped windows and concrete gargoyles as features of brutalism in Britain. These features dominate his block at the entrance to the cul-de-sac, but whereas Le Corbusier's board-marked concrete was rough, and his bricks red and crudely pointed, Stirling's block is elegantly detailed in stock brick.

The scheme was like a jigsaw puzzle. When he could not fit 30 flats in the narrow site and feared losing the job, Stirling sought advice from James Gowan, then a colleague in the firm of Lyons Israel Ellis. The success of the collaboration prompted their brief, fiery partnership. Gowan slotted two low, 'T'-shaped blocks of larger flats on to the narrow end of the site to meet the conditions of both the developer and the planning authority. Their large foyers feature concrete first-floor landings that form a bridge between glazed walls, a feature repeated by Colin St John Wilson in his own house (see page 24). The two architects also produced separate designs for the interiors of the smaller units, Stirling favouring plywood for the screen between the kitchen and dining area, Gowan solid timber and an extra radiator.

2 AND 2A GRANTCHESTER ROAD

Cambridge
1963–64; Colin St John Wilson
Listed grade II

This bold pair of houses – one for himself and his first wife and one for fellow academics Peter and Natasha Squire – was built by Wilson when he was teaching at Cambridge. The site was a former kitchen garden. The material was then novel, a Dutch concrete block introduced to Wilson by fellow architect Eldred Evans, who had planned to use the material for her unbuilt civic centre at Lincoln. The blocks allowed the plan to be laid out on a strict tartan grid 1ft (30cm) by 1ft 4in (40cm) that continues into the patios to front and rear. The two houses are similar, but Wilson's is fronted by a wing containing a studio for his practice raised over piers leading to an inner courtyard that originally featured a sculpture by Eduardo Paolozzi, later moved to the rear garden. Like his mentor Leslie Martin, Wilson sought a seamless combination of teaching and practice, with graduates staying on as his assistants. The Squires' house has a spiral stair, Wilson's a dog-leg leading to a library balcony space and an imposing double-height living room that projects at the rear in which the fireplace and gallery, all of fair-faced blocks, dominate. Wilson's friend Colin Rowe dubbed the houses 'the smallest monument in Cambridge', the most austere and classically rigorous produced by the architect before he and M. J. Long, whom he met in 1964 and married in 1972, moved decisively towards a gentler architecture inspired by Alvar Aalto and Gunnar Asplund.

HILL HOUSE

Headley, Hampshire
1970–72; Denys Lasdun & Partners
Listed grade II*

This is Lasdun's one major post-war house, intensely private and set high in the Hampshire Downs. It was commissioned by Sir Timothy Sainsbury of the supermarket family after they met at a conference in c.1964 where both were speaking on urban planning. He and Lady Sainsbury were looking for a country home that combined family accommodation with rooms for entertaining and the collection of English paintings they had begun on their marriage in 1961. Lasdun's first question was, 'How do you live?' He was working on the University of East Anglia (see page 102) at the time and first proposed a ziggurat design set into the hillside, but Sir Timothy considered the many half-landings to be impractical, and the final cruciform plan has a simple logic. The main axis has a grand double-height hall and main room for entertaining, connected by a gallery at their upper level, culminating in a giant temple front facing the valley. It repeats the grandeur of Lasdun's Royal College of Physicians, his breakthrough building, on a more domestic scale, yet its mix of in-situ concrete and concrete block appears still more monumental because of its isolated rural location. There are family rooms to either side, including a range of study bedrooms for the Sainsburys' four children, and a service range to the rear. To the west, Lasdun added a swimming pool in 1984–85 and a library – his very last building and completed in 2001 after his death.

PUBLIC HOUSING

ALTON WEST (ROEHAMPTON LANE)

Roehampton, London
1955–60; London County Council
Part listed grades II* and II

The LCC's showcase estate occupies the grounds of two Georgian villas, Mount Clare and Downshire House, restored as part of the development. That one had been landscaped by Capability Brown, then newly rediscovered, demanded a scheme that was open and imaginative. A team of young architects gathered round Colin Lucas, who fought their battles in committees and gave them a free hand; the best known went on to form the practice Howell, Killick, Partridge & Amis. The group wanted high buildings, the LCC planners more houses, and the result balances both interests. Point blocks and pensioners' bungalows were disposed to keep open views around Mount Clare. Whereas the adjoining Alton East (Portsmouth Road estate) used brick, Alton West employed storey-high concrete panels, a technological breakthrough for precasting. 'We no more wanted to work in the manner of the Portsmouth Road chaps than they would have in ours,' John Partridge recalled. The pièce de resistance was the slab blocks of narrow-fronted maisonettes developed by a larger team and based on Le Corbusier's newly completed Unité d'habitation visited by the future HKPA in 1953. Examples are found across London but nowhere else is the quality of concrete so exemplary, nor the positioning. After Harold Macmillan objected to the slabs being set in a line facing Richmond Park, they were slammed sideways into the hillside, putting their pilotis to purpose and producing one of the greatest prototypes of brutalism in London.

PARK HILL

Sheffield
1957–61; Jack Lynn and Ivor Smith, Sheffield City Council
Listed grade II*

Lynn had produced a design featuring broad access 'promenades' on every third floor for the City of London's Golden Lane competition in 1952, when Alison and Peter Smithson devised similar blocks linked by 'streets in the sky' based on the terraced colliers' housing they all knew from their native North East. Smith devised his own scheme for a student thesis, helped by the others. He and Lynn then moved to Sheffield, which in the mid-1950s was Britain's most dynamic housing authority. Park Hill dominates the city above the confluence of the rivers Sheaf and Don, where its iron industry had begun, but a centre of slum clearance since the 1930s.

The steep slope was both a difficulty and an advantage. The unique feature was that a deck could be at ground level on one part of the site and seven storeys in the air at another; only the top deck or 'row' never meets the ground. The decks were the first to be sufficiently wide for children's play and for milk floats to run along. The tough aesthetic was developed with an artist, John Forrester, who introduced graded colours of brick from plum to beige and perhaps designed the simple balcony fronts. The 13 lifts became nodal points for shops, four pubs and a laundry at their base. Unlike other giant slabs, Park Hill worked well for many years – however it declined in the early 2000s, when it was taken over by developers Urban Splash, whose first refurbishment sought to de-brutalise it. Later phases have been more sympathetic.

TOWER BLOCKS

Gilcomstoun Land, Virginia Court, Marischal Court, Porthill Court,
Seamount Court, Thistle Court, Hutcheon Court and Greig Court,
Aberdeen 1959–78;
George McIntosh Keith and (from 1970) Tom Watson, city architects
First five blocks listed grade A

Aberdeen had few problems of slum clearance or land shortages. But when its economy expanded rapidly it faced a huge demand for housing. Its response in these benign conditions was a remarkable piece of planning to a consistent programme following the 1952 report *Granite City: A Plan for Aberdeen* by W. Dobson Chapman and Charles F. Riley.

The council built suburban estates at Kinworth and Kaimhill, but also – although there was no shortage of land – eight towers in the city centre. Built in five contracts over 20 years, they follow a strikingly similar design, evolved from Gilcomstoun Land, built in 1959–63 after city architects visited Alton West in London (see page 30). All combine precast and in-situ concrete, including panels finished with chunks of granite to give local character, since painted except at Thistle, Hutcheon and Greig courts. While the ends have conventional single-storey flats, most are cross-over units on two levels, with a dual aspect. There are laundries and community rooms, and Seamount Court (1959–66) includes shops.

Gilcomstoun Land (project architect John Pressley) features the most chamfered pilotis. Subsequent blocks were mainly set in discordant pairs, the respective 9- and 19-storey Seamount and Porthill courts, and Marischal and Virginia courts, the latter angled on the imposing Union Street. Thistle Court (1971–75) is perhaps the best preserved. Last came the near-equal pair of Hutcheon and Greig courts of 1973–78, enlivening a clearance area. All add character to one of Britain's densest inner cities.

BROOKE HOUSE

Town Square, Basildon, Essex
1960–62; Anthony B. Davies, chief architect
Listed grade II

One problem with the centres of the UK's post-war new towns was that of ensuring they remained lively after the shops had shut, and of creating a landmark. The most common solution was to build flats, using the opportunity to introduce a greater variety of accommodation into the towns targeted at young professionals and the offspring of the first incomers.

Brooke House is bold. A tower 160ft (48.8m) high lights up the large town square, holding the centre between its two halves, at different levels with steps and cobbled walls until recent building work blocked the east side. The height was determined to give views across Vange Ridge south to the River Thames and ensures that Brooke House can be seen from the surrounding low hills – Basildon is much the largest of the early new towns round London. The 14 storeys are supported on 'V'-shaped pilotis 27ft (8.2m) high with a simple glazed entrance hall and a basement garage – then still novel in public housing. They are a cross-wall construction with bays of alternating widths for the living rooms, kitchens and bedrooms (bathrooms are internal next to the central corridors), formed of concrete cross-walls. Bay windows form continuous strips along the main façades, fully reversible and double-glazed, set in angled pairs to give a rippled effect. The window-cleaning gantry provides a parapet. The internal finishes of hardwood and laminated plastics was also superior to those found in most housing, as was deemed appropriate for such superior accommodation.

ARLINGTON HOUSE

All Saints' Avenue, Margate, Kent
1962–64; Russell Diplock of Diplock Associates

When Margate Sands railway station closed in 1926, Margate Corporation converted the building into the Casino dance hall, adjoining the Dreamland entertainment park. This burned down in 1946 and the site became a car park. Eventually the council turned to Bernard Sunley (1910–64), a south Londoner who became a contractor and developer after making money in open-cast mining. Best remembered for his philanthropic work, by 1961 he was already terminally ill. In March that year he agreed proposals for a shopping arcade with its own split-level car park, coining the catchphrase 'park and buy', with a scheme that resembled Diplock's designs for Brighton (see page 162). The car park serves as a podium to a 19-storey tower of luxury flats, Arlington House, its pilotis concealed within the car park. The cranked façades facing east and west give all 142 flats – eight on each floor – a view of the sea from continuous bands of glazing between precast concrete panels finished with white calcined flint. Living rooms are in the projecting sections. All the upper structure was precast, hoisted into position by tower crane. The lift foyer, set behind a long entrance hall and a concierge's lodge framed in teak, is lined in veined Carrara marble.

The car park and arcade were threatened with redevelopment as a Tesco store in 2011 in a four-storey scheme by 3D Reid. This did not happen and, while the arcade remains empty and boarded up, the car park has reopened and Arlington House's stock is rising.

VANBRUGH PARK ESTATE

Maze Hill, Greenwich, London
1962–65; Chamberlin, Powell & Bon

While Joe Chamberlin focused on Barbican and Leeds University, Geoffry Powell led on CP&B's smaller jobs. Faced with staff shortages, Greenwich Borough Council approached CP&B as a 'firm of high standing', asking them to prepare two schemes: one of multi-storey blocks, and the mixed development that was chosen in March 1960. There are three dwelling types. Most of the estate comprises two-storey terraces of houses or mews flats over garaging, built cheaply of concrete blocks with cavity walls, their subtle details now lost to replacement windows. The architectural bravura was reserved for an eight-storey tower of 64 flats, placed to give maximum views of the river and the least imposition on Blackheath. It is dominated by a sculptural lift shaft of pick-hammered concrete contrasting with large areas of glazing. There were problems with the coloured staining of the render from the first, which dried to an inconsistent brown and is now beige with a green lift top. The scheme feels like a suburban adaptation of the Golden Lane ethos and in particular the competition entry by Chamberlin, which featured low patio housing, but updated in its materials and loosened to create more open space and with the tall block more fully integrated. Powell gave special attention to preserving trees and planting courtyards and play spaces, which survive well, save for walks beneath the original block that have been enclosed. As Nicholas Taylor commented in the original *Architectural Review* article, 'children actually play here'.

BISHOPSFIELD

Harlow, Essex
1963–66; Michael Neylan of Neylan & Ungless

The new towns struggled to create an urban character since most incomers wanted only two-storey houses and gardens. In 1960, Harlow held a competition for an alternative solution, won by Michael Neylan with a scheme of flats and single-storey patio houses, where the wall of one house shields the garden of its neighbour. He exploited a low hill by building a crescent of flats over garaging at the top, from which ribbons of houses step down in narrow alleyways that earned the development its nickname of 'The Casbah'. The layout saved on roads and separated traffic from pedestrians, with wedges of grassland between the housing groups.

A smaller development followed a similar pattern at Charters Cross next door. Neylan gave his inspiration as the crescents of Kensington, but the materials are brick and concrete rather than stucco and each unit has an open space.

The aggressive design made what Neylan considered 'a recognisable and definite place [which] from the inside has a comprehensible structure'. The interiors of the houses are delightful; they are 'L'-shaped around rear gardens with open-plan living areas under high monopitch roofs. The influence of Jørn Utzon's patio housing in Denmark and Sweden is evident although, as Neylan explained, such plans were widely 'in the air', citing Chamberlin, Powell & Bon's contemporary scheme at Vanbrugh Park, Greenwich (see page 40). Two small blocks, one of bedsits, were demolished for a new road and conventional flats in 1994, when Florian Beigel carried out some refurbishment, but the scheme remains otherwise little altered.

TRINITY, ST ALBANS AND ST MICHAELS COURTS

Birley Street, Blackburn

1966–67; Cyril Fretwell (borough architect) and Sydney Greenwood

Sectra was a system of precision-made steel formwork developed in France for building large amounts of housing quickly. The formwork created tunnel-like sections across the block in room-unit widths and ceiling heights that were bolted together in rows using special tracks on the building site, before the concrete was poured to form the walls and floors in one operation. The formwork was internally heated to accelerate the hardening of the concrete in the mould, then the sections were lifted into position by tower crane. The end walls were cast in situ and often had a ribbed or relief pattern. John Laing & Son acquired the British rights in 1962 to save money on labour, using the system around the country but most extensively around Manchester and in the North West. It secured a five-year contract with the county borough of Blackburn to build three blocks per year, in a collaboration between Fretwell and Laing's in-house architect Sydney Greenwood. The 13-storey towers at Birley Street each contain 34 one-bedroom and 37 two-bedroom flats, with attached garages. Bands of precast panels across the façades feature exposed white Cornish aggregate, with panels of black Shap granite below the kitchen windows on the end walls. Screen walls at the entrances feature a relief pattern on one side and tiling on the other. Using Sectra saved less money than expected and most of its estates have now gone; this is a well-maintained group set in attractive parkland created by slum clearance.

WYNDHAM COURT

Blechynden Terrace, Southampton
1966–69; Lyons Israel Ellis
Listed grade II

Southampton expanded rapidly when in the 20th century it became the chief port for Britain's ocean liners. But while much of its imaginative public housing programme was for dock labourers on low wages, Wyndham Court was designed for professional people. Flats were leased by the year rather than rented by the week, the tenants paying far more than those on other estates but bypassing the waiting list. It occupies a sensitive war-damaged site in central Southampton, next to the railway station and near E. Berry Webber's civic centre of 1929–39. This determined the medium height of the block and choice of a near-white concrete, after the council agreed that brick was 'too suburban'. There are two floors of flats and four floors of two-storey maisonettes raised above an open ground floor on the steeply sloping site, with shops on the higher elevation facing Commercial Road, a private courtyard garden and a basement car park. The original green-painted timber windows were replaced in uPVC in the 1990s, but this did not prevent its listing, so impressive is its expression of raw power, particularly the east wing that projects on pilotis.

Edward Lyons (no relation of the better-known housing architect Eric Lyons) set up in practice with Lawrence Israel when in 1934 they won a competition for public halls at Wolverhampton. The firm specialised in schools and public buildings, but built several high-density schemes in Southampton once the city council began a slum-clearance programme in the 1950s.

ABRONHILL 4

Blackthorn Road, Cumbernauld
1967–71; Wheeler & Sproson

Abronhill, with the villages of Old Cumbernauld to the north-east and Condorrat to the west, is one of three distinct neighbourhoods that form part of the later development of Cumbernauld into the early 1970s. It stands on its own hillside, separated from the town by a deep valley, the Vault Glen, and it is the steepness of the slope that defines its most dramatic housing. A miniature version of the main town that survives in generally better shape, Abronhill has its own shopping centre, churches and three primary schools, although Abronhill High School – made famous as the location for Bill Forsyth's 1981 film *Gregory's Girl* – has been demolished.

Abronhill 4 comprises 373 dwellings, rendered and with monopitch roofs, planned as a series of four- or five-storey flats with lower terraces between. Its central east–west axis forms one of the most monumental pieces of housing design in Cumbernauld, emerging between two small towers from a flying concrete footbridge across Blackthorn Road, down a long ramp leading to a central pedestrian promenade between long rows of similar four-storey dwellings separated by an attractive lawn. The 'towers', actually no higher than the rest of the development but made imposing by their position and coloured render, shield the area from the bypass road behind. It forms a striking contrast to the one- and two-storey dwellings across the rest of the settlement.

BRUNSWICK CENTRE

Bloomsbury, Camden, London
1967–72; Patrick Hodgkinson
Listed grade II

Installed at Cambridge University, Leslie Martin retreated from building to
a consultancy role, passing work to his associates and assistants. One was Patrick
Hodgkinson, who as a student had reconfigured the London County Council's
Loughborough Estate as four-storey terraces with dual-aspect maisonettes, and with
Martin he designed similar housing for St Pancras Borough Council at West Kentish
Town, which remained unbuilt. When in 1959 St Pancras received an application
for a 40-storey office tower and three 20-storey blocks of flats, it appealed again
to Martin, but the solution was Hodgkinson's, who in 1961 designed two
'A'-shaped banks of flats over a shopping centre and car park, revised to include
an upper terrace with professional chambers when in 1963 the development was
taken over by R. McAlpine & Partners. Such terraces, known by the German term
Terrassenhaus, became fashionable following the *Visionary Architecture* exhibition
of 1961 at New York's Museum of Modern Art. However, McAlpine's sought a
conventional shopping centre with a supermarket and seeing no economic return
for the flats, in 1965 passed them to Camden. Hodgkinson resigned in 1970 rather
than see his scheme truncated by rising costs and the unavailability of part of the site
when the Territorial Army refused to budge. T. P. Bennett & Partners then scrapped
the mall's glazed cover, walkways and escalators, and left the concrete unpainted,
ignoring Hodgkinson's specification for a warm buff finish. Nevertheless, the scheme
was hugely influential on Camden's subsequent housing programme, while the
shopping centre has come to life following returbishment in 2005–08.

BROADWATER FARM

Bruce Grove, Haringey, London
1967–73; Charles E. Jacob and Salim El Doori,
Haringey Architect's Department

Broadwater Farm is a remarkably isolated development in the heart of north London, made notorious by riots in 1985 but now comfortably scruffy under layers of render and paint. It has scale rather than beauty, decent cheap housing and low crime rates.

Tottenham Urban District Council bought the Downhills Estate in 1932 to develop with recreation grounds and allotments, the latter given over to housing in the 1960s because of escalating waiting lists. The corporation adopted the Danish Larsen-Nielsen 'large panel system' being promoted by Taylor Woodrow-Anglian for its speed and relative flexibility. Though most of the blocks are four or six storeys, Haringey's architects pushed the system to produce two 19-storey towers. A late addition, designed in 1969, was Tangmere, the central ziggurat originally containing shops and a pub (the blocks are named after wartime aerodromes). Also striking were the first-floor walkways linking all the blocks, a response to the exceptionally high water table that precluded ground-floor flats. It also separated pedestrians from the ample ground-floor garaging. But so much permeability and covered space aggravated social disturbances in an area where racial tension was high. After 1985 walkways were truncated, empty shops converted, murals painted and lobbies with concierges installed in all the blocks, but more important was the careful management of the estate and the building of good community facilities. The fears in 2022 are that replacing Tangmere and Northolt (a tower with fixing problems like those that caused collapse at Ronan Point, Newham in 1968) will encourage gentrification.

AYLESBURY ESTATE

Walworth, London
1967–77; Derek Winch of Southwark Architect's Department

When the first phase opened in 1970, the Aylesbury Estate was the largest housing project by any London borough, and included the longest system-built block in Europe. John Laing & Son acquired rights to the Danish 12M Jespersen system in 1963 and opened three factories in Britain, building a pilot estate at Oldham in 1964. In Camberwell and then Southwark, borough architects Frank Hayes and particularly the Vienna-born Hans Peter (Felix) Trenton argued that central heating, more open space and a garage for every flat demanded large-scale redevelopment, resulting in more new housing than any other London borough. Their Acorn Place, Bonamy and Heygate estates have already been demolished. The Aylesbury Estate comprised 2,759 flats, covering 70 acres (28.5 hectares), the long slabs of four to 14 storeys high laid in squares following the lines of the assembly cranes and linked by walkways at second-floor level over garaging. Taplow House, one of the largest blocks, included shops (some imaginatively repurposed as art galleries or workshops) and there was a health centre and playgrounds. From the first, the architectural press criticised the poor finishes, imposed for economy, as well as the high maintenance and occupancy levels essential to maintain order. Walls along the walkway were tiled in the late 1970s to frustrate graffiti artists.

Southwark commissioned six master plans from 1995 onwards, until in 2005 Southwark Council resolved to demolish the estate piecemeal. Work began in 2008 and the western third has already gone.

CARRADALE HOUSE AND GLENKERRY HOUSE

St Leonard's Road, Tower Hamlets, London
1968–70, 1972–78; Ernö Goldfinger
Listed grade II

Poor Balfron Tower, denigrated by new windows and a remodelled internal plan, when the sensitive restoration of Carradale House next door shows what could have been done.

Carradale House was the second phase of a slum clearance scheme, begun by the Greater London Council only when residents could be decanted into Balfron Tower; keeping the old community together was as important as showcasing the advantages of living high. Goldfinger designed a 17-storey point block before preferring this 11-storey slab set at right angles to Balfron, featuring the same exemplary concrete and pattern of access galleries every third floor. These floors have small flats; those above and below have larger, dual-aspect units reached via an internal staircase, while the shared-access balcony encourages greater sociability and has faster lifts. The separation of the noisy lift tower and refuse chute from the flats is even more striking than in its neighbour.

The third phase was a 14-storey block sited so its shadow had minimum impact on its neighbours. It followed the tight 'yardstick' budgets imposed by government from 1967. The plan is similar, and the curved concrete panels are beguiling, though here combined with brick; the service tower is not detached and the counterbalancing southern tower is bulkier. In 1978 the GLC launched an experimental community scheme here, recognising the shortage of affordable leasehold accommodation in the area for key workers such as teachers. The owners' co-operative still runs the block and has ensured it is the least altered of the three.

TRELLICK TOWER

Golborne Road, London
1968–72; Ernö Goldfinger
Listed grade II*

In early 1968 Goldfinger and his wife Ursula spent two months living in Flat 130 at Balfron Tower. He promised that his testing of the room sizes, amenities and the effect of the wind would inform later blocks, but work had already begun on its west London counterpart, critically beating the government's imposition of new cost controls or 'yardsticks' for housing. It differs from its sibling in being taller, at 31 storeys, and more elegantly proportioned. It also originally included a ground-floor nursery, and a seven-storey wing featured ground-floor shops and a doctor's surgery. An intended pub at its southern end became Goldfinger's office. So many functions in one block gives Trellick Tower affinities with Le Corbusier's Unité d'habitation in Marseilles, and with a project conceived by Goldfinger on board the SS *Patris II* with the Congrès Internationaux d'Architecture Moderne back in 1933. The bridges at Trellick Tower were set on neoprene pads to avoid the transmission of noise from the service tower, in which he planned drying rooms, a meeting room and facilities for table tennis and hobbies.

Trellick Tower is only one element of the Cheltenham Estate, previously Edenham Street, the redevelopment of an area notorious for its overcrowded conditions. The scheme also included an old people's home (demolished), a six-storey block of flats, four terraces of houses and a large park. The block's fortunes were revived with the introduction of a concierge in 1983, the restoration of its coloured-glass entrance window and sensitive conservation.

ROBIN HOOD GARDENS

Robin Hood Lane, Tower Hamlets, London
1968–72; Alison and Peter Smithson

Robin Hood Gardens and the Smithsons are acclaimed around the world, save in Britain. The only public housing built by the couple, one block was demolished in 2018 for a far larger development of mundane flats.

The scheme grew out of a smaller project at Manisty Street for the London County Council, enlarged when the insanitary Grosvenor Buildings were added to the programme. The site was a traffic island adjoining the Blackwall Tunnel and the Smithsons sunk garaging behind a high wall, while thick fins, mullions and angled sills buffered noise in the flats. Living rooms face the roads, allowing bedrooms to face the inner gardens, sculpted by Alison into two great mounds using rubble from Grosvenor Buildings.

The Smithsons' unplaced entry for the Golden Lane competition in 1952 had featured wide 'streets in the sky' using linked slabs, based on the terraced streets of their native North East. Lynn and Smith then built Park Hill (see page 32), but Robin Hood Gardens adds windows and eliminates columns, as well as a vast range of flat sizes. In July 1968 the Greater London Council resolved to use the precast Sundh system for most external and partition walls, leading to awkward junctions and fixings that had to be modified further to meet new regulations introduced following Ronan Point's collapse. What is remarkable is the richness of the elevations for a precast scheme, while property guardians set to manage the surviving block before its eventual demolition are now praising the quality of the internal spaces.

DAWSON'S HEIGHTS

East Dulwich, London

1968–72; Kate Macintosh of Southwark Architect's Department

Southwark's large-scale housing blocks were mainly long, anonymous slabs, as exemplified by the Aylesbury Estate (see page 54). This is the exception, a hilltop fortress visible for miles around. Faced in 1965 with an unstable hill formed of clay excavated in the 19th century for London's railways, the chief architect Frank Hayes invited three of his assistants to prepare schemes. Macintosh was aged 26 when she proposed two staggered blocks of nine and eleven storeys as providing the most economical foundations while exploiting the dramatic views towards Hampstead Heath and the North Downs. She also believed that minimising corridors and maximising the variety of flat sizes would encourage a greater informality and sociability. The result was a poetic massing, harking back to the castles seen by Macintosh when growing up in Scotland, in which she acknowledged the influence of her engineer father and the organic architecture of Hugo Häring. Macintosh had travelled and worked extensively in northern Europe, and in 1965 had visited the Atelier 5 housing complex at Halen near Bern, which reassured her that a deep plan and reinforced concrete would work. At Dawson's Heights the exposed concrete floor slabs are contrasted with warm brick. Split-level flats, a form of scissor plan, gave most flats a view in both directions. Many are entered from ground level, important for families, and all have substantial balconies. The staggered profile, termed 'crumbly' by Macintosh, enhances the blocks' individuality and there is an underlying rhythm and proportion that makes it seem just right for its setting.

CENTRAL HILL ESTATE

Crystal Palace, London
1969–74; Rosemary Stjernstedt and Adrian Sansom,
Lambeth Architect's Department

The competition at Bishopsfield (see page 42) made fashionable two housing tropes from the Continent, the 'L'-shaped patio house and the use of a hillside to make a comfortable mid-level entry into medium-rise terraces of flats and maisonettes. The London Borough of Camden became the doyen of the latter, but one of the first examples to be approved, as early as 1966, was in Lambeth – far poorer and with the longest housing lists in London, but with some genuinely steep hills in the south of the borough. Ted Hollamby established an architect's department ahead of borough reorganisation in 1963, bringing with him many colleagues from the London County Council, including Rosemary Stjernstedt, interested in patio housing and landscape. She headed a team appointed to build at Central Hill, a north-facing slope with fantastic views across London, where tower blocks were rejected as too intrusive. Most of the 374 dwellings are terraced houses or maisonettes in four-storey blocks, accessed from the upper slope to reduce stairs and eliminate lifts; there are smaller flats over garaging and shops. Terraces of rough concrete and near-white brick form a bowl around the hillside, all with great views and most with a double aspect to bring in sunshine; all the units have a balcony or small garden. At the centre are shops, a nurses' hostel, community centre and recreation ground, with landscape by John Medhurst, who had studied under Peter Youngman. In 2017 Lambeth announced plans to rebuild the estate with 400 extra homes, many for private sale, a move stoutly resisted by residents.

ALEXANDRA ROAD ESTATE

Rowley Way, South Hampstead, London
1972–78; Neave Brown, Camden Architect's Department
Listed grade II*

Alexandra Road is the masterpiece of Neave Brown, headhunted from a teaching job at the Architectural Association by Sydney Cook, chief architect of the new London Borough of Camden. The Eyre Estate was looking to redevelop a street of large, run-down houses with luxury housing and a tower block, when in 1965 the new borough saw the opportunities of the site for social housing, without the obstructive tower.

Brown's medium-rise, high-density layout is deceptively simple. Its backbone is a curved crescent like those of Bath but containing seven storeys of flats banked up against the railway line. It shelters two lower terraces containing maisonettes and houses respectively, separated by a park also planned by Brown. The scheme fulfilled Camden's desire to separate people from traffic, with underground car parking, while also featuring workshops, a community centre and special school. It drew on the unbuilt scheme for West Kentish Town by Leslie Martin and Patrick Hodgkinson, but also on terraces from 1920s Berlin and the work of Atelier 5 in Switzerland. In the larger units, Brown set living rooms on the upper level to give maximum light, a device he had already used in an earlier terrace built privately for himself and friends at Winscombe Street, Archway. Each unit had a substantial balcony or garden. The concrete was exceptionally white and carefully board-marked, even in the park where walls separated sitting areas and playgrounds for various age groups, with planting by Janet Jack making it feel larger than it is.

SOUTHWYCK HOUSE

Coldharbour Lane, Brixton, London
1973–80; Magda Borowiecka, Lambeth Architect's Department

Magda Borowiecka was one of many architects who left the London County
Council to join the new architect's department created by their former colleague
Ted Hollamby at the London Borough of Lambeth. She produced some of Lambeth's
finest estates, notably the red-brick Dunbar Street and Clapham Manor Street
developments of the late 1970s. But she remains best known for the nine-storey
'barrier block' designed when two motorways were set to be driven through Brixton,
the elevated 'Ringway 1' or the 'motorway box', a legacy of Patrick Abercrombie's
County of London Plan revived by the Greater London Council, and an upgraded
A23 south to Brighton. While the windows on the motorway side were small, as
at Ralph Erskine's contemporary 'wall' at Byker, Newcastle, the rear elevation is
stepped to form south-facing balconies reached through large French windows;
it shelters the low-rise Moorlands Estate in its lee. The stepping and staggered,
expressed stairs came from Scandinavia, and she admitted a personal dislike of
90-degree angles – hence the canted corners.

Borowiecka got the scheme through committees and out to tender, but then
in 1973 the motorway was cancelled. John Major (the future prime minister) was
chairman of the housing committee; to have abandoned the block would have
triggered compensation payments for the tender, so he decided to go ahead.
It was set to be accompanied by a system of first-floor walkways across Brixton
town centre, of which a small part was realised alongside the Recreation Centre
(see page 234), opened in 1983.

MAIDEN LANE ESTATE

Camden, London
Phase 1, 1976–81; Gordon Benson and Alan Forsyth,
Camden Architect's Department

Maiden Lane was the last and largest of three innovative schemes by Benson and Forsyth in the London Borough of Camden's ambitious housing programme. First designed in 1972–73, it acknowledged nearby Victorian terraced houses. The site had been railway sidings, where the removal of landfill revealed a 14ft (4.3m) fall from east to west, which allowed the terraces of two-storey houses to be entered at the upper level, with a top-lit kitchen at the heart of the deep plan set over bedrooms giving on to the garden. For every two terraces there is one block of flats raised over parking. A bank to the south formed by the landfill supports a terrace of larger flats and a community centre accessed from either end, the slope used to fulfil a government requirement that family units should be at ground level.

Benson and Forsyth realised only part of their scheme. A school and nursery were dropped from the brief, as was a bridge over the railway, while informal landscaping took the place of dedicated uses for each open space. They left Camden to form their own practice in November 1979 after overseeing the completion of the first phase. What is striking is the whiteness of the concrete and its bold proportions, owing something to Le Corbusier at Pessac, which give unity across the complex levels. A second phase had to include a wider range of housing in blocks that were simpler in design and looser in layout.

CABLES WYND HOUSE

Leith, Edinburgh
1963–65; Alison & Hutchinson & Partners
Listed category A

Cables Wynd House is the 'banana block' immortalised as the home of Sick Boy in Irvine Welsh's *Trainspotting*, and now part of Leith's revival. It was the heart of the programme that saw the rebuilding of Kirkgate slums in the early 1960s. The distinctive curved shape was a response to the awkward site, creating a barrier to the street on one side and providing some shelter for balconies and a garden on the other. All 212 flats have a balcony set within the in-situ concrete frame. The broad access decks on the second, fifth and eighth floors also serve the intermediate floors, following an adventurous pattern designed to give sociability by placing more front doors together, but also greater privacy to the flats on the intermediate floors. No bedrooms were set next to the deck, while with fewer stops the six lifts also became faster and more efficient. Adopted by only the most progressive authorities, the plan's ultimate source was the Narkomfin building in Moscow, but Park Hill, Sheffield (see page 32) provided a closer model.

Edinburgh was unusual in that its most imaginative housing schemes were provided by private architects (based in the city) rather than a public architect's department. Alison & Hutchison & Partners became large-scale housing specialists under Robert Forbes Hutchison (1908–76), who had been chief architect to the Regional Hospital Boards of Scotland and so understood the value of improved sanitation and facilities. Here he worked with Walter Scott (1926–2010), who formed his own practice in 1964.

EDUCATION

SCHOOL OF ARCHITECTURE EXTENSION

Scroope Terrace, Cambridge
1958–59; Colin St John Wilson and Alex Hardy
Listed grade II

When in 1956 Leslie Martin became professor of architecture at Cambridge, he invited Wilson to teach and practice with him. Martin tended to explore his ideas by collaborating with associates, assistants and acolytes, of whom Wilson was the most important; this building, however, was Wilson's own, with Hardy providing the services and their students producing design studies and many of the final drawings. The expanded school of architecture needed a lecture room, with below it a space for criticism and student design reviews ('the pit') and four tutorial rooms. The geometry follows the golden section on a square 1ft 6in (46cm) grid but is realised in yellow brick around exposed concrete slabs and beams. It is indebted to Stirling and Gowan's flats at Ham Common but also the classical theories of Rudolf Wittkower, with elements like the lecture rooms' centrally pivoted doors taken from Le Corbusier. The ground floor features built-in concrete seats and a servery for coffee in an off-centre service cube resembling the fireplaces at Ham Common; in the lecture room the slide projectors were mounted on a concrete pulpit cantilevered from this core. The ceiling beams and louvres are also exposed, as is the rough concrete stair in the glazed link between the new building and the 1830s terrace facing the street. Le Corbusier and Henry Moore were both in Cambridge to receive honorary degrees, and Martin invited them to inaugurate the building in June 1959 with a joint lecture. The building survives remarkably little altered.

CHURCHILL COLLEGE

Storey's Way, Cambridge
1959–68; Richard Sheppard, Robson & Partners
Listed grade II

Churchill College wears its board-marked concrete comfortably, like the rough greatcoat of its namesake. The Second World War had revealed the deficiencies of science education in Britain, and Sir Winston Churchill was one of those anxious to address the problem. The project for a new men's college at Cambridge focusing on the sciences received generous funding from industry and trades unions. It is a physical symbol of the importance of pure sciences in the atomic age and a memorial to Churchill, whose archives are held here. A college panel of experimental scientists oversaw every stage of construction, duly antagonising the architects. The palpable feeling of design by committee contrasts Churchill with Arne Jacobsen's single vision at St Catherine's, Oxford, but reaffirms the sense that its more brutalist envelope can accommodate greater flexibility.

Leslie Martin, professor of architecture at Cambridge, invited 21 firms to produce designs in the post-war's most important competition for a building that spoke of its age. Sheppard's team, led by William Mullins, won the two-stage process in 1958–59 with a clever interpretation of the traditional Oxbridge quad. Its structure of concrete frame and brick infill equally suited the grand gesture at its entrance, the great arch-vaulted dining hall and the study bedrooms. The competition was also important for heralding young firms like Howell, Killick, Partridge & Amis and Stirling and Gowan, bringing them university commissions elsewhere in Cambridge, Oxford and beyond – as too it served the Smithsons, Architects' Co-Partnership and others with schemes in this book.

FALMER HOUSE

Sussex University, Falmer, Brighton
1960–62; Sir Basil Spence & Partners
Listed grade I

Brighton's proposal in 1956 for a new university at Stanmer Park coincided with a recognition that more young people were seeking higher education, and set a model for a generation of new universities. The seven established in England looked for ways of building quickly and economically in ways that expressed their large science departments and encouraged cross-fertilisation between the arts and social sciences courses.

Spence was asked to prepare a master plan for an initial 800 students, with room for expansion. Mindful of Robert Adam's quadrangle at Edinburgh University, he focused on a courtyard building where teaching and recreational facilities could be concentrated while building works went on all around; it remains the focus of the campus. The style, however, was that of Le Corbusier's government buildings at Chandigarh. Spence also claimed to have been inspired by a visit to Rome, where the ruined arched construction of the Colosseum impressed him. He and his young assistants produced a quadrangle of concrete vaults with walling of local brick and flint, with some vaults left open to give views through to the Downs, reflecting the concern for landscape that had earned him the job. Shallow reflecting pools, originally set outside as well as within the courtyard, affirmed the tranquil mood. The result is one of Spence's toughest but most individual works. Two principal spaces remain little altered: the refectory, dominated by a mural by Ivon Hitchens, then living nearby, and the former debating chamber in a projecting wing to the north.

ENGINEERING BUILDING

Leicester University
1960–63; James Stirling and James Gowan
Listed grade II*

Is this the most important post-war building in Britain? It signalled the abandonment of mid-century Scandinavian influences for a more aggressive architecture, albeit one based on British engineering history and European expressionism. It responded to a complex brief by the young professor Edward Parkes. There was little land and tutors' offices remained in the main university building, making space for large ground-floor laboratories, their top-lit glazing set diagonally by Gowan and the engineer Frank Newby since the plot does not run north–south. Aerodynamics and electrical engineering were raised over the service areas as they required less heavy equipment and partly overhang the road, which importantly enabled equipment to be hauled through floor openings from lorries parked beneath. Other accommodation had to be set in two towers, linked by staircases, the taller one providing the necessary height for a water tank to power the large hydraulics laboratory, with in between two lecture theatres and four postgraduate research labs.

The red brick, tile and north-light glazing owe something to Leicester's traditional single-storey workshops, many visible in the extensive panorama from the upper floors. They are Accrington brick and Dutch tiles, but their colours feel right; the palette of brick, concrete and tile is repeated internally. The placing of the tower's supporting columns at the chamfered corners, based on 'Y'-shaped trusses devised by Newby, enabled the upper parts to be clad with patent glazing on all eight sides. This was poorly renewed in the 1980s; later renewal of the laboratories' ply-glass rooflights was much better.

FORMER UNIVERSITY OF MANCHESTER INSTITUTE OF SCIENCE AND TECHNOLOGY

Altrincham Street, Manchester
1960–66; Arthur Gibbon of Cruickshank and Seward

The most coherent complex of post-war buildings for higher education in Manchester was built for its college of technology, raised to university status in 1964 and an autonomous body until 2003. It is not strictly brutalist, but it has just enough wilful geometry to give character and it is dense, intense, compact and multi-layered.

The centrepiece is the Renold Building, the first dedicated lecture block in an English civic university, designed in 1958 and built ahead of that at Leeds (see page 96). The college found that it was more economical to build a single block of top-notch theatres that could be shared by the various departments, creating at the same time a place where students could meet. The idea of a space to 'see and be seen' extends to the fully glazed stair tower as well as a large entrance with a mural, *Metamorphosis*, by Victor Pasmore, also designed in 1958 but not executed until 1968. The saw-tooth glazing pattern was designed to limit sound penetration. Across the sunken gardens – exploiting the basements of demolished warehousing – is the Barnes Wallis Building, the former students' union and a hall of residence with a distinctive rooftop funnel that lights the stairs. Most dramatic is the 15-storey Mathematics and Social Sciences tower, where shuttered concrete comes to the fore. Behind the unexceptional Moffat Building of 1967 is a sculpted boundary wall by Anthony Hollaway, formed of prefabricated textured panels slotted into concrete columns, the one listed element of the complex.

ASHLEY AND STRATHCONA BUILDINGS

Birmingham University
1961–62; Howell, Killick, Partridge & Amis
Listed grade II

The critical praise for HKPA's entry to the prestigious Churchill College competition at Cambridge (see page 78) brought the nascent practice its first jobs. One was for St Anne's College, Oxford, the other at Birmingham University, where Casson & Conder had produced a master plan for expansion in 1956 and brought in a range of leading modern architects to produce a mix of buildings on the lines of MIT or Yale in the United States. The merger of the Faculty of Commerce with the Honours School of Economics and Social and Political Science produced a teaching body as rambling as its name, housed in a series of huts. New buildings were needed to bring the elements together, so Bill Howell designed the five-storey Ashley Building, housing 69 tutorial and staff rooms arranged around an open atrium under a domed roof. It was served by a single continuous staircase designed to foster chance meetings and sociability. The lower Strathcona Building, containing seminar rooms and a lecture hall, shielded the department from traffic noise on the adjoining ring road.

HKPA's work for the London County Council at Alton West (see page 30) had pioneered the use of full-height precast panels. Here a fully reinforced concrete structure proved too expensive and load-bearing brickwork had to be partly substituted. Instead the complex saw the firm's first use of smaller panels incorporating projecting windows (designed to throw dirty rainwater off the building), which resemble the squares of a chocolate bar.

DENYS WILKINSON BUILDING
(NUCLEAR PHYSICS)

Banbury Road, Oxford
1962–71; Philip Dowson of Ove Arup & Partners

Cambridge University led Oxford in science, and under Ernest Rutherford led the world in nuclear physics. In the early 1950s Denys Wilkinson studied the breaking down of atoms by their acceleration at very high voltages and realised that a tandem accelerator with a horizontal and a vertical electrostatic generator could create the necessary voltages. However, money for such a machine was only available to the Atomic Energy Research Establishment near Oxford. Wilkinson duly moved, then looked to build a machine that could be used by his students. His chance came with changes in government funding, his passionate campaign securing a grant in 1961.

Jack Lankester, Oxford University's surveyor and an enthusiast for Danish architecture, proposed Ove Arup & Partners, engineers with an architect's section experienced in designing laboratories. The task was to incorporate the vertical accelerator tower within a building of moderate height. Dowson shielded it by placing it in the angle of the teaching block containing laboratories and a flat for Wilkinson, slightly separating it since he recognised it might have a short lifespan. A comparable horizontal accumulator filled the basement. They were decommissioned in 1997, when research moved to Geneva.

The tower's funnel shape was determined by its function; a glazed centrepiece between flanking shields reduces the appearance of bulk. Dowson was masterful in detailing concrete to avoid staining, here with vermiculated and ribbed patterns. The building led to the formation of Arup Associates as an independent multi-disciplinary practice.

STRATHCLYDE UNIVERSITY

Glasgow

1962–72; various architects

School of Architecture and Wolfson Building listed grade B

Glasgow's second university received its charter only in 1964, though it can trace its origins to the 1796 Anderson's Institution and already had an inner-city site near the cathedral. New buildings, mainly for social sciences, followed on the steep hill to the south-west around Rottenrow and south to George Street in a master plan by Robert Matthew. Earliest is the McCance Building of 1962–63 by Covell Matthews & Partners, which combines lecture theatres and a library (featuring murals by William Mitchell) with shops and first-floor parking. Next to it, the Livingstone Tower of 1965–68 was originally commercial offices for British Telecom. A more elegant group behind centres on the former Department of Architecture from 1964–67 (remodelled in 2019–21 as the Learning and Teaching Building) by the university's own professor, Frank Fielden. This is of blue engineering brick with projecting bays clad in copperised felt and a row of north-facing rooflights articulating the former studios where every student was allocated a permanent space in an office-like environment. Next to it is the John Anderson Building for Natural Philosophy, an 'L'-shaped slab by Building Design Partnership of 1968–71 and the monumental serrated block of the Wolfson Centre for Biological Engineering of 1969–72, a surprisingly brutal venture by the normally cool modernists Morris & Steedman. In the angle at the top of a green quadrangle that cuts through Rottenrow is *Callanish* by Gerald Laing, also from 1971, inspired by the stone circle on Lewis but colloquially known as 'Steel Henge' for its use of Cor-ten steel.

ACLAND BURGHLEY SCHOOL

Burghley Road, Tufnell Park, London
1963–67; Howell, Killick, Partridge & Amis
Listed grade II

The London County Council promoted comprehensive schools over selection at age 11, but these schools had to be big to realise a viable sixth form. Yet since the only sites in central London were very small, classrooms, workshops and laboratories had to be packed on top of each other, producing daunting expositions in reinforced concrete, whether designed in-house or passed to an approved list of private architects based in London. This is architecture designed for hard knocks. Part of the site of Acland Burghley (named for the two board schools it replaced) was set over a railway, where only complex engineering made it usable for a playground and games hall. For the rest, the ambitious but socially aware first headmaster L. A. Abley determined that the school should be divided into year groups rather than houses 'like them public schools have', to make the school appear smaller and more welcoming, particularly to younger students. The fortress-like teaching block accordingly has three wings: an upper, middle and lower school designed around the need for efficient circulation at the transfer between lessons, with a lower administrative block. The concrete frame is clad with precast panels finished in flints. To the side, a semi-detached assembly hall bears witness to the school's specialism in drama and dance, and its board-marked finishes are softened by a lantern roof of real timber boarding, described by HKPA's biographer Geraint Franklin as 'almost a theatre with a school attached'. An open-air amphitheatre is the principal landscape feature.

HAGGERSTON SCHOOL

Weymouth Terrace, Hackney, London
1963–67; Ernö Goldfinger
Listed grade II

Goldfinger's only secondary school was originally built for girls. It is a balancing act of strong shapes, their proportions based on a 16ft 6in (5m) grid and multiples of π, with the entrance block and hall one of his most complete compositions. The materials are strong: Staffordshire blue brick and concrete, with Corbusian gargoyles. The doors, inside and out, have their own concrete surrounds. Inside are stone flag floors and coffered concrete ceilings to the long circulation space, an elegant staircase and gallery leading to first-floor offices and a textured brick wall in the main hall designed for acoustic absorption. Delays in casting the coffered roof deck (which ensured the main hall required no columns) meant the block opened a year late and was not widely published.

London's large comprehensives had to squeeze a vast range of accommodation on to small sites. They typically feature a hall block, a main teaching range and separate gymnasia. Goldfinger first set his classrooms, six house rooms and a library in two blocks, but then refined the composition as a single, more elegant and economical spine range, the larger rooms projecting. This was the first part to be completed, in 1966. It was remodelled in 2010–12 with new circulation and fenestration by Avanti Architects, who as part of the conversion to co-educational use added a new range for art and technology inspired by Goldfinger's little caretaker's house to one side. Goldfinger also designed the hard landscaping of granite setts across the site.

LEEDS UNIVERSITY ADDITIONS

Leeds, West Yorkshire
1963–78; Chamberlin, Powell & Bon
Listed grade II and II*

Leeds University grew more rapidly than any other in the 1960s. Appointed master planners in 1959, CP&B's proposals were ground-breaking for their detailed research. They found that most departments needed lecture theatres only part of the time, so recommended a series of flexible departmental buildings based around a block of shared theatres. The stepping and servicing of these variously sized spaces gives the Roger Stevens Building (grade II*) its form.

The scale of the venture approaches CP&B's Barbican Estate in scale. Yet only one quadrangle was fully realised, Chancellor's Court, with the senior common room to its west and the physics building to the east. Large blocks for biological sciences opened to the south in 1968; a library was added northwards in 1973–75 and a social sciences' building in 1978. These long slabs of glass and concrete were delineated by pairs of beams, on a strict grid with service ducts between them, so that laboratories and tutorial rooms could be altered as needed. Rainbow colours denote the floors and level pedestrian routes through the buildings connecting the central lecture theatres, from the Red Route starting at the top of the hill and becoming a high-level walkway, to the Purple Route linking the lower southern buildings to the equally brutal Worsley Medical and Dental Schools by BDP (1979). CP&B also built student flats to enliven the campus, using traditional red brick to contrast with the concrete teaching buildings; these survive at the Henry Price Building of 1963–64 by Christoph Bon.

DUNELM HOUSE
(STUDENTS' UNION)

New Elvet, Durham
1964–66; Richard Raines, Architects' Co-Partnership
Listed grade II

Dunelm House has been a major conservation battle for the Twentieth Century Society since it was threatened with demolition in 2016. The University of Durham resolved in 1963 to build a social centre for its growing number of students scattered in colleges and bedsits around the city and beyond. The site was determined by the Kingsgate Bridge being built by Ove Arup & Partners across the gorge of the River Wear due east of the cathedral. The same engineers worked on Dunelm House, creating a contrast between the open form of the high-flying bridge and the solid mass of the students' union cascading down to the water. Arup is commemorated by a bust on the side of the building, but it was a young American, Richard Raines, who gave Dunelm House its mix of classical proportions and a brutalist aesthetic after studying under Peter Smithson at the Architectural Association.

The concrete is formed of lightweight foamed slag aggregate with board-marking, the windows set behind rhythmic patterns of concrete mullions. Because it was so visible from the bridge, the Royal Fine Art Commission chose a special roof covering of interlocking slabs resembling giant Roman tiles, specially funded by the Treasury. Inside, a broad staircase descends straight to the river, with wide landings on each level serving the café, bars and ballroom. Thelonious Monk performed at the opening concert in spring 1966. Dunelm House was finally listed in 2021 but its future remains uncertain.

HISTORY FACULTY

Sidgwick Avenue, Cambridge
1964–68; James Stirling
Listed grade II*

With interest growing in the firm following their design for Churchill College (see page 78) and the engineering building under way at Leicester (page 82), Stirling and James Gowan were invited in December 1962 to enter a competition for a history faculty. This was part of a complex of arts buildings masterminded by Casson & Conder. The design was substantially Stirling's and the partnership split the next year. The centrepiece is the great Seeley Library, its glass roof inspired by 19th-century reading rooms. The impact comes from its large volume, easily supervised fan-like section and exposed roof structure, with lines of books on a gallery round the edge. It is bookended by two blocks at right angles, housing an ascending order of common rooms, seminar rooms and tutors' studies, accessed by ramps to a podium as well as from the ground floor. The building occupies a pivotal place in Stirling's oeuvre, in which his synthesis of Le Corbusier's Maisons Jaoul with industrial England's red-brick tradition was first tempered by a symmetry inspired by Antonio Sant'Elia, then being rediscovered.

The building quickly became controversial because the glass roof caused overheating. This was blamed on its reorientation through 90 degrees after the university failed to secure part of the site, though actually this made no difference. Air conditioning was too expensive, and an innovative ventilation system was abandoned as too noisy. In 1980 falling tiles from its façades led the university to consider demolition, before Bickerdike Allen Partners conducted repairs in 1985–86 using matching red brickwork.

UNIVERSITY OF EAST ANGLIA

Norwich
1964–68; Denys Lasdun & Partners
Listed grade II* (ziggurats) and grade II (teaching wall and library)

Lasdun was commissioned in 1962 to produce a master plan and the first buildings for this new university, the third after Sussex had opened the way for new foundations. A large site was chosen alongside the River Yare, from which a lake was formed only in 1975–77. Lasdun was determined to preserve this open landscape, and placed his buildings where the valley starts to rise.

Lasdun's aim, like Chamberlin at Leeds, was for a 'five-minute university' with departmental buildings and residential accommodation close together. He thus proposed a long teaching spine flanked by student flats, with a library in a central green 'dry dock', all linked by high-level walkways. The cranked spine also symbolised the links between subject areas where academic research was concentrating in the 1960s. The concrete construction combined in-situ work with panels precision-cast on site, in-situ service towers projecting from Lasdun's distinctive, crisply finished and very long horizontals.

Student flats were cheaper and considered more progressive than traditional halls, with 12 students sharing a kitchen/diner, creating a supportive social grouping equivalent to the Oxbridge staircase. Each flat is set back and partially lowered so that its sill level meets the roof of that below. This stepped section and continuous profile, with each block at 90 degrees to the next, has led to the terraces becoming known as the ziggurats. Only two lines of ziggurats were completed before Lasdun's contract was terminated in 1968, but they remain the boldest architecture in any new university.

UNIVERSITY OF ESSEX

Wivenhoe Park, Colchester

1964–72; Kenneth Capon of the Architects' Co-Partnership

Essex was architecturally the most ambitious of the seven entirely new universities founded in England at the turn of the 1960s. This was due to the vice-chancellor, Albert Sloman, who had taught at the vast Berkeley campus of the University of California and worked closely with Capon before other appointments were made. The site was a river valley set in beautiful parkland, which they sought to preserve by building a compact central campus, but one for 20,000 students – then an exceptional number for a British provincial university. The teaching buildings were wound round a series of podiums raised over the valley, permitting services and parking underneath. This encouraged the students to mix, and large departments to expand and contract within the continuous slab of tutorial rooms and laboratories. Only a lecture block, library and restaurant stood out from the mass, set where the podiums met the slope of the hillside. Beyond them were 14-storey blocks of student flats, the tallest towers in Britain built of loadbearing brick, chosen for economy and viable because no large spans were needed. There was no collegiate structure; Sloman saw his students as mature adults, yet this relative freedom may have provoked Essex to become a centre of unrest in the 1970s. He and Capon planned 31 towers, but only six were built. Work stopped in 1972, leaving the megastructure incomplete but in splendid isolation. Large additions since 2000 have sprawled across the surrounding landscape, diluting Capon's concept of an Italian hill town.

ASSEMBLY HALL

Bootham School, York
1965–66; Trevor Dannatt
Listed grade II

Trevor Dannatt gave brutalism a human face. Coming to prominence as an assistant on the Royal Festival Hall, his mature style evolved in a collaboration with Leslie Martin at College Hall, a hall of residence for women at Leicester University. Bootham School, a Society of Friends' public school, sought an assembly hall that would hold its own in a traditional setting: it was conceived as a piece of sculpture to sit in the foreground in views from the school's Georgian buildings towards York Minster.

Dannatt had a Congregationalist upbringing and there is a modesty, calm and simplicity to his buildings; his brother became a Quaker. Importantly this was his first collaboration with the engineer Ted Happold, a Bootham old boy with whom he subsequently worked extensively. The Bootham hall was Dannatt's favourite of his buildings, in which elements of his university work with Martin are more boldly expressed. The concrete is board-marked, inside and out; a staircase is expressed like a crouched reptilian leg. The double-height auditorium can be used for meetings, or for sports and theatre – its flat floor can be partly raised to form a forestage, and stage lighting is concealed in its central clerestory. On two sides a gallery is lined in elm boarding and fitted with fixed benches. A screen of elm boarding can conceal the stage when required. The hall is no longer freestanding: a music and arts complex was added in 2012–14 by Squires and Brown.

LECTURE THEATRES

Brunel University, Uxbridge, London
1965–67; John Heywood of Richard Sheppard, Robson & Partners
Listed grade II

A Clockwork Orange's plot-shifting Ludovico Medical Facility was in reality Brunel University, Britain's first wholly new university dedicated to science and engineering. Acton Technical College had already moved to Uxbridge, where it looked to create a landmark in the heart of featureless suburbia before being re-founded in 1966. Its planning group visited the University of Manchester Institute of Science and Technology (see page 84) before similarly placing the main lecture theatres in a single block. The raked floors and fire escapes of the six large lecture theatres became architectural features, made fashionable by Leicester's Engineering Building but here treated on an epic scale across a single façade. They form a giant north-facing wall of board-marked concrete, the upper flight of theatres projecting on giant columns and beams, with the technicians' cubic booths projecting still further. Inside the theatres share a triple-height atrium that also serves smaller facilities to the south, including a special room for music.

Richard Sheppard and Geoffrey Robson made their reputations with Churchill College, Cambridge (see page 78). An earlier Corbusian exercise was an addition to Imperial College, London University's principal scientific campus, which was largely demolished despite being listed. But their most brutal experiment was Brunel, where they produced the master plan and shared buildings, with Stillman & Eastwick-Field designing specialised laboratory and workshop blocks for engineering and applied sciences in four linked towers of dark brick and concrete. The core of this little campus remains much as Stanley Kubrick would have known it.

UNIVERSITY OF BATH

Bath

1965–80; Hugh Morris of Robert Matthew, Johnson-Marshall & Partners

Of all universities, the University of Bath most closely resembles a dense hill town comparable with Cumbernauld. It comprises a central square (The Parade) of libraries, refectories and shops on a raised podium flanked by departmental buildings and student flats. Whereas RMJM's contemporary University of York (see page 112) was a series of lightweight structures strewn round a picturesque lake, Bath is enclosed and heavy, though also built of CLASP – a prefabricated system developed for Nottingham schools (see page 122), but here a special version using concrete as well as steel for multi-storey dwellings. The non-collegiate character is most evident in the nine-storey and six-storey blocks of flats, the first phase completed in 1970. To the south the main square opens out to a small lake. Like Brunel, it grew out of a college of advanced technology, so budgets were tight, and the structures had to support heavy engineering equipment.

The complex has been much extended, so now the scruffy new town is lost in an academic suburbia. The exceptions are by Alison and Peter Smithson, who realised their last works in Britain after Peter secured a teaching job here in 1969. They imagined their small additions as tassels to RMJM's carpet, rather than individual buildings. Most important is 6 East, the Department of Architecture and Civil Engineering of 1982–88 in concrete block, with some Bath stone and proportions that nod to the city's classical traditions. Its key features are the route created between the main car park and bus terminus through to the central square and, internally, informal spaces where students could share ideas.

CENTRAL HALL AND LIBRARY

University of York
1966–68; Robert Matthew, Johnson-Marshall & Partners
Listed grade II

The University of York was among the most picturesque of the new universities established in the early 1960s. RMJM's master plan, by the partner Andrew Derbyshire, established a series of small colleges and larger science buildings around a settling lake, created because of the flat site's high water table and crossed by a series of covered walkways. Its centrepiece is a hall for lectures, examinations, sport, concerts, drama and conferences that sits at the greatest bend in the lake.

Whereas most of the buildings adopted a lightweight prefabricated system, CLASP, developed for Nottinghamshire schools in mining areas, the largest and most complex structures like the hall and library were built of in-situ reinforced concrete. A suspended mild-steel tubular roof clad in aluminium ensures there are no columns in the raised first-floor hall, which has raked seating for 1,250 people on three sides formed around a removable sectional stage, orchestra pit and flat central floor. Yet it is the exterior that impresses, with the raked seating expressed as a series of steps that reflect the ripples of the water above the glazed ground-floor foyers. The concrete was painted in 2004, but this has not diminished the hall's power – surprising in the lush landscape setting that unites the various buildings of what is now West Campus. A covered walk and concrete bridge lead uphill to the library, the route punctuated by an untitled sculpture of 1967 by local sculptor Austin Wright in its own concrete courtyard.

ANDREW MELVILLE HALL

North Haugh, St Andrews, Fife
1966–68; James Stirling
Listed grade A

Encouraged to expand, St Andrew's University needed halls of residence to be built quickly, and commissioned James Stirling after an academic committee visited new university buildings in England. Unusually for Stirling, the clients remained friends – despite problems with leaking windows and poor heating.

Andrew Melville Hall comprises two fingers stretching out towards St Andrew's Bay, angled to give each study bedroom a view of the hills beyond. Initial plans for rectangular rooms and cranked corridors gave way to a straight spine and cranked rooms. It was the first in a sequence of very linear buildings by Stirling, and the first to be prefabricated. He claimed that there were no local contractors, nor even bricks, so concrete panels were manufactured in Edinburgh. Their diagonal ribbing was inspired by the Leicester Engineering Building (see page 82), where in-situ surfaces were ribbed to take tiles; here it controlled staining. Three-inch (7.5cm) margins permitted easy handling and crisp corners. Had the six more fingers planned by Stirling been built there might have been economies in scale; the excessive cost of the first pair ensured this did not happen.

The site was a former cliff face stranded when the sea receded. The main entrance was originally at the rear (altered in a careful restoration of 2018), where a path led into town. Thence study bedrooms spill down the slope as well as up staircases from a promenade the length of the building at this level. At night this illuminated deck enforces the impression of an ocean liner moored at harbour.

FLOREY BUILDING

23–24 St Clements Street, Oxford
1968–71; James Stirling & Partners
Listed grade II*

The last of Stirling's 'red trilogy' and perhaps the most controversial today, the building is a memorial to the provost Howard, later Baron, Florey. His sudden death robbed the project of its leader before building began, leading to a change of brief from graduate accommodation to provision for undergraduates. The site was intended for a controversial road, and the neighbouring buildings were set to be demolished; Stirling turned his back on them and created a horseshoe towards the river. It resembles his unbuilt scheme with James Gowan for Selwyn College, Cambridge, an amphitheatre of glass, red brick and tile where each storey jetties forward in the manner of Marcel Breuer's project of 1928–29 for Elberfeld Hospital, making space for circulation at the rear. Twin towers for stairs and a lift anticipate the formal, symmetrical entrance at his Sackler Museum at Harvard University in the United States (1979–84). A top-lit breakfast room is enlivened by a weathervane to direct the kitchen ventilator away from the prevailing wind to prevent smells. Provision was made for a public path by the river only partly realised and leading only to awkward fencing.

The building has always attracted a range of responses, with problems of overheating, cold bridging and overlooking. The residents must respect the omnipresence of the architecture, whether a column projecting through a room or the striking redness of the tiles. Potentially damaging proposals for its extension were approved in 2016 before its listing was upgraded, but since then it has stood empty.

INSTITUTE OF EDUCATION AND SOAS LIBRARY

Bedford Way, Bloomsbury, London
1970–76; Denys Lasdun & Partners
Listed grade II*

Lasdun had come to prominence with his masterpiece, the Royal College of Physicians, a testament to his supreme logic of design with its tight organisation of materials and spaces. Built a decade later, the Institute of Education reworks many of its ideas, a product of his mature years when his language of strata and towers had become more dominant but budgets were far tighter.

The University of London commissioned Lasdun in 1960 to develop the concept of a spinal range along Bedford Way that had been published by Leslie Martin and Trevor Dannatt the year before. His task was to integrate new buildings for law and education within a network of Georgian squares that were coming to be appreciated. Lasdun preserved more of these terraces than had Martin, and created a new square facing his library extension for the School of Oriental and African Studies, much of it raised over basement lecture theatres. For him, the relationship between his two buildings was paramount. He intended that the spine should have five spurs projecting into the square, but only one was realised. The elevations contrast bands of glazing and bronzed aluminium panels with sturdy concrete lift towers, all raised on a chamfered plinth, and a deliciously over-scaled escape stair steps down the spur. Inside, Lasdun's exemplary attention to fine concrete is best seen in the lift lobbies, and above all in the walls and balustrade to the principal stair leading down to the lecture theatres.

119

DE BREYNE AND HAYWARD BUILDINGS

Keble College, Blackhall Road, Oxford
1971–73, 1975–76; Ahrends, Burton and Koralek
Listed grade II*

Casson & Conder produced a master plan in 1968 for extending Keble College on its island site, with study bedrooms, two flats, a bar and graduate common room. ABK secured the commission in 1969 for new buildings, after failing to persuade the college to retain the 19th-century houses on the site and link them by a sunken covered walkway. 'They wanted to make a statement,' said Peter Ahrends, the partner in charge. The difficulty was to design a building that could stand up to William Butterfield's apotheosis of high-Victorian Gothic brutalism.

Ahrends's eventual solution was a snakelike structure, beginning with a spiral staircase in the highest part of the building and which uncoils down Blackhall Road. He likened the pattern of blind walling and projecting piers along the street to those of Albi Cathedral, while flowing forms became a hallmark of his work within the firm. The angled brick plinth was another distinctive feature, also found at the Oxford Catholic Chaplaincy, again by Ahrends. To the rear, the block steps down to a sunken walkway retained from the initial scheme, but is otherwise entirely glazed. The honey-coloured brick and angled black glass offer a sophisticated coolness juxtaposed against Butterfield's fireworks. Comparisons can be made with James Stirling's red-brick and glass Florey Building (see page 116), but ABK's tinted glass, northerly aspect and good ventilation ensured there were fewer problems of overheating. Listing, however, did not prevent the tip of the snake's tail from being demolished for a new block by Rick Mather.

SIXTH FORM COLLEGE, CHILWELL SCHOOL

Queen's Road West, Chilwell, Nottinghamshire
1975–76; CLASP/Nottinghamshire County Council Architect's Department
Listed grade II

Whereas prefabrication for housing proved controversial, it offered great advantages of speed and flexibility for building schools. Nottinghamshire County Council developed a lightweight system in 1955–56 as a solution to mining subsidence as well as shortages, combining a light steel frame and tile or concrete claddings that could be used for most public buildings. On its adoption by other mining areas, it became the Consortium of Local Authorities Special Programme (CLASP). The programme was expanded to build large comprehensive schools, sports complexes and even the University of York, as well as buildings abroad. As the buildings got bigger, so the cladding panels became larger and more sophisticated, culminating in the early 1970s as the metric CLASP Mark 5.

Nottinghamshire often combined its large comprehensive schools with community sports facilities, as at Chilwell. To ease the transition from primary schools, these complexes included a separate building for 11–13-year-olds. As was briefly fashionable in the 1970s, much of the building was open plan for ease of communication and supervision. In the 1980s it became a sixth-form centre, which found this open plan ideally flexible for teaching small groups and so, unusually, it survives. CLASP was rarely elegant visually, deliberately so in the hands of its technically minded chief architect Henry Swain, but here the job architects Michael Tempest and Roger Bearsmore responded to the lakeside setting and used the limited palette of panels and oriel windows to advantage. Inside the central staircase in the double-height, top-lit atrium is particularly finely detailed.

ARGOED SCHOOL

Bryn-y-baal, Mynydd Isa, Mold
1977–81; George G. Tomlinson, Clwyd County Council

Argoed is a delicious confection of bold angles and impertinent corbels executed in unadorned concrete, despite all efforts to clutter it with new windows, signs and a post-modern entrance extension. Precision concrete and neat, expressive detailing such as gargoyles combine with bands of patent glazing and asbestos roof tiles, with much play made of slots, recesses and small projections so that water falls away rather than causing stains. It is the boldest secondary school left in Wales following the demolition in 2006 of Bettws High School by Evans & Shalev, though its own days are numbered. The classroom windows are angled to catch the light just like those in John Bancroft's celebrated Pimlico School, also demolished, and some have a similarly double-backed plan. These were built first, in 1977–78, to be followed by a kitchen, dining room, music room, staff rooms and a youth club. It was the first purpose-built school for 11–14-year-olds, built when Clwyd County Council experimented with a middle-school system of secondary education.

George Grahame Tomlinson (1921–2020) succeeded Robert Harvey in 1977 as county architect for Clwyd, the combined authority for Denbighshire and Flintshire created in 1974. He continued his forebear's bold brutalist aesthetic, which fits surprisingly well into the area's mix of deep countryside, mining towns and (as here) suburbia. The high school is set to be demolished when a new all-age school for the area is completed – it is due to open in 2023.

PUBLIC BUILDINGS

SALTASH LIBRARY

Callington Road, Saltash, Cornwall
1961–63; Royston Summers, Cornwall County Council
Listed grade II

Many small towns and rural areas had no permanent library until the 1960s.
A report in 1959 called for more expenditure on buildings as well as books,
leading to the opening of 350 new libraries across Britain by 1965. In Cornwall
there was an extreme contrast between older towns, where in the 19th century the
journalist John Passmore Edwards had endowed many libraries, and dormitory
communities such as Saltash. The county architect, Kenneth Hicklin, set out to address
the problem by building a series of regional centres, intended as hubs for smaller
facilities and mobile van services. The first, at St Austell and Newquay, were mid-
century modern in style, faced in traditional stone. Then came Saltash, by Hicklin's
assistant Royston Summers (1931–2012). Like the earlier libraries, it comprised a
single, double-height hall with a gallery for reference and non-fiction titles, but as it
was intended as the focus of a new civic centre (never built) a monumental design
was allowed, its façade indebted to the upswept frontages of Le Corbusier's state
buildings at Chandigarh, India – notably the Palace of Assembly then also under
construction. It was not thought appropriate to explain this to the councillors; instead
an exceptionally eloquent committee report extolled the beauty of reflected sunlight
from a nearby pool and justified the butterfly roof as allowing cross-ventilation from
clerestory windows. The result was nevertheless called the most Corbusian building
in Britain. Summers set up his own practice in London in 1964, specialising in
housing and energy efficiency.

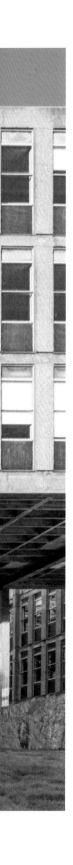

LYS KERNOW
(NEW COUNTY HALL)

Truro
1963–66; F. Kenneth Hicklin, Cornwall county architect
Listed grade II

Hicklin's most important task as county architect was to extend the modest Edwardian county hall (now flats). His proposals dwarfed the old building and the council agreed to build a new county hall on a site recommended by Geoffrey Jellicoe; initial drawings are jointly credited to Jellicoe and Hicklin. Cornwall's is a granite landscape, with few buildings of brick, and heavy concrete and render fit in well – aided by a substantial cement industry in the county.

Only the first phase was completed. Lys Kernow is a bold, quadrangular building appropriate to the large landscape. A sharp fall in the ground permitted two storeys to be tucked into the hillside, although most of the rear elevation was left open at ground level, the upper floors supported on giant pilotis. The projecting council chamber is distinguished by Derbydene limestone cladding, with granite aggregate and Delabole slate used elsewhere; broader windows denote the council suite. Jellicoe produced plans for the landscape, left as open as possible save in the central courtyard. While the exterior was brutal, the cool interior reflects the suavity of Arne Jacobsen, whose town halls Hicklin and his assistants visited in October 1960, and features works by local artists. The quadrangle includes Barbara Hepworth's *Rock Form (Porthcurno)*. However, in mid-1963 the councillors attacked Hicklin for buying furnishings from national suppliers rather than Cornish contractors. Hicklin retired rather than fight these local interests, and his talented young team dispersed – ending Cornwall's brief reign as a centre of modern public architecture.

BUCKINGHAMSHIRE COUNTY OFFICES

Walton Street, Aylesbury
1963–66; F. B. Pooley, county architect

A feature of the 1960s and 1970s was the building of giant county offices to bring large departments on to one site, which created problems since nearly all were in historic towns. That for Buckinghamshire was one of the first and best, a 13-storey landmark that can be seen for miles around, but which resembles a modern castle keep. It was developed in conjunction with a new road network and relates to the small neo-Georgian county hall of the 1920s across Walton Road.

Later in his career, Pooley wanted to be remembered as the begetter of Milton Keynes and for challenging prefabrication in schools and libraries, where he encouraged a neo-vernacular revival in the 1970s. But for the county's own offices he and the job architect Malcolm Dean were unashamedly brutalist, creating large, semi-open-plan offices behind a new central library designed to fit into the largely two- and three-storey street (a contrast with older buildings now lost with the building of a new library next door). Most of the construction was precast, an economical and technically accomplished solution, with in-situ concrete at the end lift/stair bays to tie the construction together. Groups of bay windows on the upper floors lit the architect's and planning departments, most notably the architects' drawing boards, which were given a prime spot at the top of the building. Meeting rooms were set in the corners. Less successful was the circulation at the entrance, set round a courtyard that was altered in the 1990s

NUFFIELD TRANSPLANTATION SURGERY UNIT

Western General Hospital, Edinburgh
1964–68; Peter Womersley

Hemmed into the corner of a busy hospital, this little building announces itself by its honey colour and a contorted profile of beams and ducts. Womersley spoke of 'an attempt to express the idea of ducting'. Ducts dominate the building, for this was the world's first sterile unit for kidney transplants, led by Professor Michael Woodruff and a model for later units elsewhere. Womersley secured the job in 1963 through John Holt, chief architect to the regional hospital board, who had earlier commissioned a psychiatric unit at Haddington. The building had to be totally air-conditioned, with a sterile zone for six patients held in near isolation for over five weeks. Service ducts above and below the zone had to be accessed without contacting the patients, and Womersley treated these pairs of half-curved beams as brackets that grow out of the building and articulate its many separate layers. Air intakes and ventilation extracts repeated the theme as towers. The patients, trapped between 'clean' and 'dirty' corridors, looked out on to an observation area and thence to the outside world; these few larger windows are cantilevered over a semi-basement. A corridor to the main building led to a radiotherapy department, an ultimately unsuccessful way of treating organ rejection.

The concrete is marble-smooth, cast in situ against fibreglass. The ochre cement was chosen to match the stone gable-end wall of the adjoining building but is more strident. The entrance hall featured semi-circular vaults in the ceiling formed from the same moulds as the ducting.

SOUTH NORWOOD LIBRARY

Selhurst Road, Croydon
1966–68; (Henry) Hugh Lea, borough architect

Pity Hugh Lea, trained in Leeds, who rose from obscurity with the County Borough of Croydon to lead the team of architects in the enlarged borough from 1965 and thence to head a new architect's department. Big-thinking Croydon was the first borough to build a tower block as its own offices, Taberner House by Lea and Harry Thornley – but this has been demolished, while Lea's public baths in South Norwood have been altered. That leaves what Bridget Cherry called his other 'borough showpiece', South Norwood Library. But this too is threatened with demolition.

The library is a small building on a busy road, easily dwarfed by late 19th-century neighbours. So Lea made its elevations bold, constructivist in their shapes with big windows in aluminium frames contrasted with a blind upper storey facing Selhurst Road. The concrete panels were precast with a pebble facing that was then incised to reveal the concrete beneath. Best of all is the bronze signage in a personalised Gothic bold condensed font. The plan exploited the steep site, setting the main lending library down the hillside so it can be made double in height with a gallery. Placing most books in a gallery allowed flexibility in the main space for a range of activities. What is more unusual is that the children's library occupies the mezzanine to the front, behind the sign, while the basement was given over to the reference area, a means of giving small children maximum light and fewest stairs.

CHORLEY POLICE STATION AND MAGISTRATES' COURT

St Thomas's Road, Chorley, Lancashire
1966–68; Lancashire Architect's Department, county architect Roger Booth

Lancashire County Council had one of the most extensive post-war building programmes outside London, and under Roger Booth – the county architect from 1962–1983 – developed an exceptional programme of prefabrication for the vast number of schools, libraries and police stations required for a county that until 1974 stretched from Warrington to Barrow-in-Furness and included many small towns with inadequate public amenities. Booth had served in the Royal Engineering Corps in the Second World War and this informed his technical approach to architecture. However, when Chorley offered the chance to create a unique combination of police station and magistrates' court, linked at basement level and forming a three-sided square with the Victorian town hall, his team produced two one-off designs. The strong horizontality of the six-storey police station, with its exposed in-situ concrete floor slabs, contrasts with the vertical fins of the more elegant two-storey magistrates' court. The unequal pyramids on the latter's roof, clad in copper, express the two courtrooms within. Otherwise the materials were dark brick and light concrete, relieved by relief panels screening a semi-basement car park and small garden. To the rear more garaging, in lighter brick, gives the semblance of a podium. As Booth moved towards standardisation and a kit of parts, the police station was essentially repeated at Bury in 1969 (with the addition of a basement nuclear bunker and rifle range, all now demolished) and at Leyland in 1971. The magistrates' court closed in 2019 and has still to find a buyer.

HYDE PARK BARRACKS

Knightsbridge, London
1967–70; Sir Basil Spence & Partners

When Spence was commissioned in 1959 to rebuild the squalid Victorian cavalry barracks adjoining Hyde Park, his fame was at its height. The brief was to provide accommodation for the Household Cavalry, their families and horses, on a long but narrow and tapering site. The scheme was delayed by the Profumo Affair before being resolved as six contrasting sections ranging from the two-storey stables at one end to the elegant officers' mess and quarters at the other. In between was a parade ground, a barrack block, the other ranks' mess, a riding school and a 33-storey tower containing married quarters. Spence had to combine decent housing with the ceremonial traditions of the cavalry regiments. The finishes had to be tough, to withstand so many men and horses, but also to reflect their military bearing; Spence declared that 'I did not want this to be a mimsy-pimsy building ... It is for soldiers. On horses. In armour.' The precast elements were based on the ribbed finishes of Twickenham Bridge, cast and then struck by hammers, with board-marked concrete and red brick which acknowledged that of nearby mansion blocks. Spence and his assistants paid most attention to the tower, intended to relate to a group then being proposed at the top of Sloane Street, where they sought to introduce as much glazing as possible. The corona-like top contains squash courts. So large a complex in so sensitive a location contributed to a backlash against Spence in the 1970s, but it well deserves reassessment.

POLICE STATION

Bonny Street, Blackpool

1968–72; Lancashire Architect's Department, county architect Roger Booth

Blackpool Central Station, the busiest in Britain in 1911, closed in 1964 for redevelopment after the borough council persuaded Dr Beeching to retain Blackpool North instead. The valuable central site was to be part of a new development on a raised deck leading from Blackpool Tower to courts and a police station. Tom Mellor & Co. designed single-storey magistrates' and county courts, which perch on top of three storeys of car parking with elegantly canted balustrading. Recession stymied Blackpool's plans thereafter, so it was left to Booth to pursue his programme of standardisation, begun at Chorley (see page 138), with an 'Elemental Design Approach' and a system of precast storey-high concrete panels that he christened his 'Heavy Concrete Method'. The aggregate was carefully chosen to approximate the Portland stone of the court buildings, with the panels themselves given a roughly textured finish. Further police stations using the panel system followed in the mid-1970s at Morecambe, Preston, St Helens and Skelmersdale. The windows are narrow slits, save on the upper floors, giving a fortress quality. Staggered ranks of square planters on the pedestrian deck add a slightly surreal, sculptural quality to the fixed seating, while sunken landscape gardens brought light into the lower floors.

Bonny Street Police Station closed in 2018 and is set to be demolished following the opening of new headquarters at Marton. The wedge of land between the Golden Mile and Central Drive is set to be redeveloped with new recreational activities, including a 'thrill and gaming zone'.

GWENT HOUSE

Gwent Square, Cwmbran
1969–73; Richard Sheppard, Robson & Partners

The plans for a commercial hub at the heart of Cwmbran new town from the first included a central building containing a range of leisure facilities. After visiting rebuilt Rotterdam in 1958, the head of the development corporation, Lady Rhys Williams, determined that a 'really fine building' was key to the success of the new town. Following her resignation in 1960, the project stalled until the appointment of a new general manager, James McComb, in 1962 and a new, young chief architect, Gordon Redfern from the London County Council. A protégé of Graeme Shankland and a keen socialist, Redfern finally realised the large pedestrian shopping centre, including a 22-storey residential block ('The Tower') and Monmouth House, built in 1965–67 with 56 flats to bring life to the area after the ground-floor shops shut, featuring a relief by William Mitchell.

    For the town's most prestigious building the corporation in 1966 appointed one of London's leading specialists in public buildings. An intended hotel never materialised and belatedly McComb recognised the need for office jobs in Cwmbran. Gwent House included offices – initially occupied by the corporation itself – as well as shops, banks, the flexible 500-seat Congress Theatre and a public library. The precast concrete cladding on a 20ft (6m) grid reflected the discipline established by Redfern. Facing Gwent Square are murals by Henry and Joyce Collins at first-floor level featuring figures from across the area's history: a Welsh tribesman, a Roman centurion from nearby Caerleon, a medieval cleric and a miner.

HOVE TOWN HALL

Norton Road, Hove
1970–74; John Wells-Thorpe of Gotch & Partners

The social heart of residential Hove was the vast concert hall built as the centrepiece of its Victorian Gothic town hall. Until, that is, in January 1966 it burned down and the councillors determined to rebuild the whole complex in modern materials, turning to a local architect with whom they had worked previously.

The key elements were a great hall, banqueting room and car park. However, members of the buildings committee visited new civic centres at Hemel Hempstead, St Albans and Truro, as well as the Queen Elizabeth Hall and Congress Theatre, before approving Wells-Thorpe's design. Councillor Donald Edmonds declared it 'beautiful and brilliant ... a building which is not in any way grandiose and does not overshadow the neighbourhood'. Visitors might differ. The architect explained how he had created 'an interesting skyline and silhouette'; the new building was to have a clock but not the giant bell tower of its predecessor. Handsome finishes include bronzed aluminium glazing that contrasts with board-marked in-situ concrete and striated precast panels finished in Derbyshire spar aggregate. The interior combines concrete with wych-elm panelling, while the great hall has an acoustic ceiling like a cubist egg crate. The council chamber was designed with a flat floor so it could be adapted to other uses if plans for local government reorganisation in 1974 meant it was not needed, and it was one of Britain's first buildings to be given an award for its disabled access.

CIVIC OFFICES

Dunning Street, Middlesbrough

1971–73; A. P. Armitage, Teesside Borough Architect's Department

Middlesbrough was a hamlet of four farmhouses, until in 1831, Joseph Pease created a port, expanded when iron ore was discovered nearby. G. D. Hoskins's grandiloquent town hall of 1883–89 became its centrepiece, its great height made possible by concealed iron construction.

By the 1970s, when Middlesbrough was briefly capital of the county borough of Teesside, more offices were needed. Armitage and his assistants J. A. Parkin and R. A. Stephenson, working for the borough architect John V. Wall, added an 'L'-shaped range to the south and east, its second floor linked to the first floor of the old building, such was the latter's height. The new work is of its time as assuredly as the old, save for the steep-pitched roof. Unusually for Teesside the structure is concrete, set outside the building line to minimise the number of columns within and to frame and shield the large windows. The other unusual feature is its dark colour, thanks to a mix of Whinstone fines and blue Shap aggregate chosen to give 'dignity' and contrasted with brown brindle brick for the end elevations and lift shaft.

The thick amber float glass in the windows filters solar radiation and reduces glare. Beneath them are infill panels of toughened plate glass, ceramic-coated on the rear face to blend with the amber appearance. The fenestration pattern reflects the open office plan, then innovative, with each bay intended to accommodate a small working team with maximum flexibility. A second phase was never realised.

NORRISH CENTRAL LIBRARY

Guildhall Walk, Portsmouth
1972–76; Ken Norrish and Michael Gill, City Architect's Department

Portsmouth, dominated by the Royal Navy, did not get the great libraries and museums endowed by glory-seeking businessmen found in northern cities. A modest central library was bombed, and for a time a replacement was planned in the Tricorn Centre, which might have provided valuable footfall. Instead the city librarian, Ralph Mabron, secured his own building in a civic square laid out to a master plan by Lord Esher – a striking piece of pedestrian planning partly on the site of the Southern Railway's goods station. But whereas new council offices by Teggin & Taylor are an elegant dichotomy between high-tech bronzed glazing and a concrete frame, the library designed by Norrish and Gill under the city architect William D. Worden is a full-on piece of brutalism. This is especially true of the entrance, where similar bronze glazing is flanked by two staircase towers in ribbed concrete. The real surprise is to the side, where a pedestrian bridge leads to law courts (a museum was planned and never built).

We know something of Norrish's taste in buildings, since he left his extensive book collection to the library, and it included several volumes on Frank Lloyd Wright; he had also visited the Guggenheim Museum shortly before preparing his design in 1970. The bowed elevations shade the continuous windows from direct sunshine, in a fashion begun by Marcel Breuer's Elberfeld Hospital. But Norrish's curves are just that bit fatter than Wright's, more irregular and touchingly more organic, in part due to the warmth of their mosaic cladding.

SWANSEA CIVIC CENTRE

Oystermouth Road, Swansea
1979–84; C. W. Quick, County Architect's Department

How quickly buildings become redundant! When local government was reorganised in 1974 and the county of West Glamorgan formed, an attempt to share Swansea's Art Deco Guildhall quickly failed. Amid protests at rising costs and the loss of late Georgian houses in a prime location, Quick produced an elegant design that hugged the waterfront, working under the chief architect James S. Webb. The building belies its great size by being divided into three wings, two of which cradle the council chamber, a pod above the main entrance. Quick made the best of simple materials, using bands of calcined flint panels contrasted with bronze glass. Built in two phases, the first opened in 1982, winning a Concrete Award in 1983. The assessors considered that 'it demonstrates that a prestigious building in an exacting climatic situation can be very attractive in concrete when the architect's careful detailing is supported by excellent framework and casting on the part of the contractor'.

West Glamorgan County Council was abolished in 1996 and the building passed to Swansea City Council, who made alterations in 2008 when it was renamed and the central library moved in. In 2016 came proposals for its demolition, confirmed in September 2021 when the council appointed Manchester developers Urban Splash to deliver a new 'mixed-use waterfront centre' rather than the mix of old and new that has worked so well in the repurposing of the city's extensive former harbour.

SHOPS, MARKETS AND TOWN CENTRES

RINGWAY CENTRE

Smallbrook Queensway, Birmingham
1958–60; James A. Roberts and Sydney Greenwood

Post-war Birmingham was masterminded by its city engineer, Herbert Manzoni, whose greatest legacy is the inner ring road that scythes through the centre. The first section, begun in 1957 ahead of most other cities, ran from Smallbrook Street to Carrs Lane, replacing war damage. To either side Manzoni blithely leased sites to developers without consulting his architect's department. He welcomed a proposal from a developer of Polish origins recently settled in Birmingham, Jo Godfrey, the only man to propose making the first three sites into a single coherent scheme. His architect was a dynamic local buccaneer with big ideas, James A. Roberts, who later built the Rotunda tower near New Street station. On Smallbrook Queensway he conceived the ribbon-like, six-storey Ringway Centre, then considered the longest shopping frontage in the country, with shops, offices, a Mecca ballroom, car park and service area. Across the road he set the Albany Hotel. Because of Godfrey's relative inexperience, Manzoni persuaded him to collaborate with the investment division of John Laing & Son, which had also produced a scheme. Their architect Sydney Greenwood introduced the precast panels, a Laing's speciality, and curved uplighters in concrete, intended to flood the building in waves of changing colour. The large scale means that the concrete panels establish their own rhythms of light and shade and permits any amount of brash signage without disrupting its overall grandeur. The shops and parking precluded Queensway from becoming a clear expressway, a mistake not repeated in later stages of the ring road.

TOWN CENTRE

Cumbernauld
1962–67; Geoffrey Copcutt, Cumbernauld Development Corporation

Cumbernauld is the greatest new town in Britain, full of innovation and interest.
Designated in 1955 to relieve overcrowding in Glasgow, it sought a greater urbanism
than had been realised in the first new towns, which epitomised low-density suburban
planning. The site was a long, ridge-like hill, and the chief architect-planner Hugh
Wilson planned a core of housing surrounding a single massive building serving as
the town centre at its crest, linked by pedestrian paths and served by a separated
dual carriageway running beneath it. Wilson visited American shopping centres in
1961, but entrusted the design to his deputy Geoffrey Copcutt, who took the idea
of an indoor centre to its greatest extreme, piling shops, a banking court and public
functions into a multi-layered edifice topped by a library, offices and penthouse flats.
Its layers were most evident on the south side, stepped in terraces facing the sun,
but now partially demolished and blocked by the conventional Antonine Shopping
Centre built against it in 2006–07. The Golden Eagle Hotel has gone, as has the
sense of a broad square linked to Gillespie, Kidd & Coia's adjoining technical
college. The north side, with its strung-out precincts (e.g. for banking) meeting St
Mungo's church in a small square, survives better, as do the upper parts of the
casbah-like interior. Cumbernauld chimed with ideas then emerging on buildings for
growth and change, shaping the megastructure and ideas on traffic planning, and
was the first indoor town centre anywhere to offer more than shops.

BEACON TOWER

St John's Precinct, Liverpool
1963–70; James A. Roberts & Partners
Listed grade II

Liverpool's economy was ailing by the early 1960s with the decline of its docks, and in 1962 the city appointed the innovative planner Graeme Shankland to remodel its central area. He found that the corporation had already agreed with the developers Ravenseft to build an indoor shopping arcade on the site of its central wholesale and retail markets, with James A. Roberts of Birmingham as its architect. The resulting St John's Precinct came to dominate his master plan, a forerunner of the city's Liverpool One venture, with at its heart a boiler flue 409ft (125m) high.

From his holidays, Shankland sent the planning team a postcard of the Euromast in Rotterdam, built in 1960, hinting that it should be a model for encasing the boiler flue as a prospect tower, offering 'new vistas in merchandising and entertainment techniques'. The resulting 146-seat restaurant, 380ft (116m) in the air, was opened by the Lord Mayor in May 1970, signalling the culmination and completion of the £10 million precinct. It revolved once every 20 minutes, promising views of Wales on clear days. The restaurant closed in 1979 and later became a radio station, when a floor was added that blocked its rotation. The tapering main shaft, containing two high-speed lifts, was built in situ using a proprietary slipform shutter system that gives it a powerful yet elegant grace. What also impresses is the tower's relationship with the circular additions made in 1966–68 by Hall, O'Donahue and Wilson to the Victorian Liverpool Playhouse at its base.

CHURCHILL SQUARE AND TOWERS

Brighton

1963–71; Russell Diplock Associates; 1965–67, 1966–68;
Richard Seifert & Partners

Slum clearance in Brighton? The corporation had been considering redeveloping land south of Western Road since the late 1930s, when Russell Street and Blucher Place were demolished, though the Cannon Brewery survived into the 1950s. Further clearances followed at Artillery Street and Cannon Street in 1957–58 but the council prepared its final scheme only in 1959, with Hugh Casson acting as consultant. In January 1963 it won a public inquiry for a 15-acre (6ha) redevelopment including the Kingswest and Brighton Centre sites towards the sea. Kingswest and the Russell Street car park were the first elements, and the initial phase of a new shopping centre followed in 1965–68. A multi-level section of shops followed to the south in 1971–72 and filled with chain stores, sparing the small shops in The Lanes and North Steyne.

The shops were rebuilt in 1995–96, when William Mitchell's fountain sculpture, *Spirit of Brighton*, was lost. What survives are three car parks and Chartwell Court, an 18-storey block of flats built in 1967–71 above the Cannon car park for builders Taylor Woodrow. The original plan included a second block of similar height and a 30-storey block on the seafront. Instead Richard Seifert & Partners designed two towers, the 24-storey Sussex Heights on the site of St Margaret's Chapel and the slightly earlier Bedford Tower, a six-storey hotel replacing the fire-damaged Bedford Hotel (now Holiday Inn) with 11 storeys of flats on top. Also worth a visit is the spiritualist church in Edward Street by Bev Pike of Overton & Partners, 1964–65.

NORCO HOUSE (JOHN LEWIS)

George Street, Aberdeen
1966–70; Covell Matthews & Partners

This was the space-age department store of Aberdeen's Northern Co-operative Society, replacing smaller shops in George Street and Gallowgate. Its three upper floors are clad in ribbed concrete panels, each with just a narrow-glazed clerestory strip. It took until the 1960s for architects to realise that department stores were better dark, with displays lit artificially. The first floor overhangs the pavement to make a canopy, but those above are progressively set back in pyramidal fashion. The panels wrap round their curved profile, including the soft corners, like the giant treads of an airport conveyor belt.

The Northern Co-operative Company was formed in 1861, inspired by the Rochdale Pioneers, but it remained independent of the Co-operative Wholesale Society and employed its own architects. This was the first use of the name 'Norco', which the society then adopted for all its subsequent operations until going into receivership in 1993.

There was originally a strange outlier to the south: a single-storey Norco food hall set under a triangular turret and boiler flue. When the store was sold to John Lewis this was demolished and replaced by a bland extension and a glazed link to the Bon Accord Centre (1987–90 by Jenkins & Marr), reopening in 1989. Historic Scotland considered Norco House to be of listable quality but declined to recommend designation because of an outstanding planning permission for major works. John Lewis resolved in March 2021 not to reopen the store after the Covid pandemic, so its future is uncertain.

ANGLIA SQUARE

Magdalen Street, Norwich
1966–71; Alan Cooke & Partners

Brutalist megastructures swept away old streetscapes and underlying archaeology only for historians to ruminate longingly on what has gone. Nowhere is this truer than at Anglia Square, site of Saxon Northwic but largely occupied by a Victorian crepe mill before German Baedeker raids focused on historic cities in 1942. The 1945 Norwich Plan determined on an inner ring road, and the clearance of remaining buildings in the early 1960s set the way for a short cut here, with a flyover above Magdalen Street that gives access to an upper level at Anglia Square and a multi-storey car park, closed in 2018. Below are shops, with above it an office block, Gildengate House. To the west is Sovereign House, offices for HMSO opened in 1968, its spiral staircase clad in steel and glass a contrast to the surrounding concrete. To the east lies the thousand-seat Odeon Cinema opened in 1971, replacing an Art Deco predecessor. As the three-screen Hollywood Cinema, it premiered *Alan Partridge: Alpha Papa* in 2013; there is a mural of Partridge/Steve Coogan.

Sovereign House closed in the early 2000s and the cinema in 2019, but rebuilding plans approved in 2007–09 were never implemented, and a scheme including a 20-storey tower was rejected in 2021. New proposals feature 1,100 flats, but less parking and retail than their predecessors and no cinema. Meanwhile, the shortage of cheap retail space in Norwich means that Anglia Square remains resiliently open, while Gildengate House has become home to start-up enterprises, young artists and a gym.

INDOOR MARKET

Middleton Grange Shopping Centre, West Hartlepool
1967–71; Clifford Culpin & Partners

In 1948 the County Borough of Hartlepool engaged the enigmatic master planner Max Lock to survey the old town and its Victorian extension, West Hartlepool. He found that the many small shopping parades and corner shops were struggling, so proposed a single major shopping centre at Middleton Grange in the heart of the Victorian town, centred on Victory Square. It included a new pedestrian high street with to one side an indoor market, replacing a tall red-brick Victorian market on Lynn Street (demolished in 1975). The shopping street and central square were roofed over and extended in 1992 so they now dominate the striking market building in a manner not intended.

Clifford Culpin was the son of a London county councillor and worked extensively with Labour councils; here, unusually, there was no developer. He later built a new civic centre for the town. Culpin and the engineers A. E. Beer & Partners raised the market hall over ground-floor car parking, exploiting a natural 12ft (3.7m) fall of the land across the site. A walkway leads from Victoria Road to the main first-floor precinct, which leads in turn to the slightly separated market hall, with small permanent shops round its edge. The effect is dramatic, a movement from dark to light thanks to five enormous rooflights. They are formed by a series of cranked reinforced-concrete beams carried by long-span cross beams that are in turn supported by concrete walls like five enormous sails – very appropriate for a maritime town.

Eyelashes, Eyebrows & Nails

VICTORIA CENTRE

Milton Street, Nottingham
1967–72; Arthur Swift & Partners

Nottingham Victoria was the magnum opus of late railway building, a white elephant from its opening in 1900, but a beautiful station set deep in a cutting scythed through the city. It closed in 1967 and only the clock tower and Station Hotel (now the Hilton) survive. In its place arose Nottingham's first indoor shopping centre and one of the first in Britain, five times larger than Birmingham's Bull Ring and the largest commercial development in Britain by a wholly private operation outside London. It was a city within a city. There was Tiffany's disco below, and above the shopping centre are five slabs containing over 400 flats as well as offices.

Job architect Peter Winchester claimed to be inspired by Sergei Kadleigh's scheme for building over the tracks near Paddington Station from 1952. His perspectives show a space-age atrium bursting with ramps and galleries. A more prosaic two-storey shopping mall won out – an avenue of shops with a bus station at one end and anchor stores at both. However, the concrete of the columns and balustrades was satisfyingly gnarled and egg-crate lighting kept deliberately dark to focus attention on the boutiques that fuelled the teenage Harwood's lust for fashion. Rowland Emett's clock fountain, the *Aqua Horological Tintinnabulator*, still plays – though on the quarter-hour from the upper deck. Below, the cutting is filled with three floors of car parking, but the Mansfield Road railway tunnel remained visible and alluring until blocked by the most recent extension.

QUEENSGATE MARKET HALL

Huddersfield
1968–70; Gwyn Roberts of the J. Seymour Harris Partnership
Listed grade II

Queensgate Market is a dramatic ensemble of architecture, engineering and art, listed in 2005 after the loss of many 1960s markets. The corporation leased a large town-centre freehold to the developer Murrayfield, who worked extensively with Labour councils, and used the same architects to rebuild its own Victorian market hall. The roof structure is based on 21 paraboloid umbrella-like shells, designed asymmetrically to permit north-light clerestory glazing after Roberts, the project architect, visited Félix Candela's warehouse for John Lewis at Stevenage. The different heights of the umbrellas at Huddersfield developed by the engineer Joe Nicholls of Leonard & Partners make the structure distinctive, for the board-marked shells cantilever further to one side than the other, striking in their repetition. There were originally 187 stalls and 27 shop units, with a glazed first-floor café at the heart of the design, long closed. The south elevation, facing the ring road, announces its presence with nine reliefs, *Articulation in Movement*, by the émigré sculptor Fritz Steller that claim to be among the largest ceramic sculptures in the world. A tenth, still larger, was added in 1972 when the adjoining shops were completed. They were inspired by the mushroom shells, turned through 90 degrees. Steller also produced a mural in black-painted steel for the interior, *Commerce*. He met Roberts when they were both at college in Birmingham. Since 2018 the market has been partly occupied by Temporary Contemporary, a platform for contemporary art and music but no substitute for commercial vitality.

KIRKGATE ARNDALE CENTRE

Bradford

1972–76; John Brunton & Partners with Percy Grey

Victorian market halls occupied large central sites owned by city councils, so became prime candidates for redevelopment as part of the commercial expansion of the 1960s. Few councils were keener developers than Bradford's, whose architect W. Clifford Brown secured contracts for John Poulson, head of Britain's largest private practice; both were convicted for corruption in the early 1970s. News that the contract for Kirkgate's redevelopment was going to Poulson's clients, the developers Mount St Bernard, was leaked and local rival Sam Chippindale, co-founder of Arndale, stepped in. The centre, built in two phases, forms the heart of Bradford's shopping district: a cruciform plan of air-conditioned shopping malls on two levels that meet in a double-height square. It featured a new market hall as well as pubs and restaurants, with rooftop car parking accessed from the top of the steeply sloping site. It won a European award in 1979 from the International Council of Shopping Centres.

In 1954 John Brunton took over the local practice of Samuel Jackson, which he had joined 20 years earlier. Like Richard Seifert in London, he made much of his wartime service (in the Royal Engineers) to court clients and established a solid team of proven commercial designers. He retired in 1979 but the practice continued until 1992. The Kirkgate Centre has been refurbished internally but the exterior remains a powerful composition. It also retains abstract mosaics, plus three works by William Mitchell in a rare figurative style (also adopted for a Stevenage underpass, 1972).

RIVERGATE CENTRE

Irvine, Ayrshire

1973–76; John Billingham in succession to David Gosling, chief architect

David Gosling had worked at Runcorn, expanded as a new town with a multi-storey indoor shopping centre at its very heart. Appointed as chief architect to Irvine he again inherited a plan for an indoor shopping centre, this time slung on a deck over the River Irvine as a giant bridge thrust into the old town centre. It was an attempt to bring together the commercial hub on the east side of the river with the railway and harbour on the west, while traffic was diverted on to a new ring road. The consultant planners Hugh Wilson and Lewis Womersley likened the scheme to the inhabited bridges of medieval Europe. The corporation brought in private developers Ravenseft Properties and Murrayfield Scotland in 1970 to realise its commercial potential, with Ove Arup & Partners the engineers. The concrete structure was clad in white glazed tiles and curtain walling in black anodised aluminium. To the east it was set to link with new offices, Bridgegate House, the redevelopment of a congested traffic junction. At the same time, the corporation looked to restore the 19th-century red-stone Trinity Church, already derelict for ten years, as its counterpoint.

The shopping centre was extended in 1986 and again in 1998, yet it remains dramatic. It never fulfilled its original aim of linking up with the railway station and a new leisure centre in the harbour (since replaced by a new building in the middle of the town).

177

WORKS
OF ART

MURAL

Town Square, Basildon, Essex
1958; Geoffrey Clarke

Basildon had one of the first pedestrian town centres and a commitment to public art that has gone unacknowledged. A fountain by Maurice Lambert survives but mosaics by William Gordon and Anthony Hollaway have gone, and a sculpture by A. J. Poole from Freedom House, demolished in 2019, is in storage. Geoffrey Clarke worked primarily as a sculptor and designed glass at Coventry Cathedral; Basil Spence had a consultancy role at Basildon and may have provided a connection. Clarke also produced a mural for Spence's physics building at Liverpool University, but this is slightly earlier.

The mural is set in a concave projecting bay three storeys high, set above a covered arcade. It was designed to be viewed from across West Square, before Marks & Spencer's was built in 1971. The abstract design of angular forms, whether branches or sparks of electricity, was painted by Clarke, approved in April 1958 and pieced together by his wife, Ethelwynne 'Bill' Tyrer. The block of shops and offices, threatened with demolition in 2022, are by Lionel H. Frewster for Ravenseft Properties, the leading commercial developers who moved into the new towns after dominating rebuilding in blitzed city centres such as Hull and Bristol.

Geoffrey Clarke (1924–2014) was one of the group of artists who exhibited at the Venice Biennale in 1952, whose work was christened 'the geometry of fear' by Herbert Read for its mutant overtones of the nuclear age. Such work brings together elements of Art Brut and nascent brutalism.

CHEQUES
CASHED
INSTANTLY

CHEQUES
CASHED

CA$H
MART
WE BUY WE SELL WE LOAN

CASH
LOANS

RETAINING WALL, KNOWSLEY HEIGHTS

Primrose Drive, Huyton, Merseyside
1962–63; Anthony Hollaway

When it came to the decorative treatment of concrete, Bill Mitchell's nearest rival was Anthony Hollaway (1928–2000), the two coming to prominence when they shared a job at the London County Council. The housing architect Oliver Cox secured them a year's contract there to create artworks on its new buildings at modest cost, bringing a closer relationship between artists and architects than was possible when a sculpture was simply bought in. Hollaway often worked in mosaics, ceramic fragments and hardwood set in resin, but also explored ways of decorating concrete – as at Huyton. Knowsley Heights features a long 650ft (198m) retaining wall by the engineers Ove Arup & Partners as part of a development by Liverpool City Architect's Department under its chief architect Ronald Bradbury, approved in 1961. It wiggles round an open space, its curves contrasting with 11-storey towers on the hillside above. The shapes were cut from expanded polystyrene and fitted inside the shuttering before the concrete was poured. One of the three blocks was demolished in 1987, when the remaining pair were overclad (leading to a fire in 1991 now seen as a portent of Grenville Tower), but the wall with its simple, shallow reliefs survives well.

NORTH PECKHAM
CIVIC CENTRE

Old Kent Road, London
1964–66; Southwark Architect's Department with Adam Kossowski
Listed grade II

Frank Hayes had already established a progressive architect's department for the Borough of Camberwell (including Peckham) that formed the core of a team incorporated into the expanded London Borough of Southwark in 1965. The civic centre is a four-square yellow brick box containing a double-height theatre, now used as a church, which rises from a darker plinth that originally housed a library. The extensive basement contained a car park, loading bay and bookstore, maximising the steep fall in the site towards the Surrey Canal, then still operating.

The theatre provided lively entertainment into the 1990s, ranging from a local pantomime to new theatre and comedy from Lily Savage. Ghost marks of its affectionate moniker, 'The Civic', can still be detected on the main elevation. It is most remarkable today, however, for Kossowski's sequence of tile murals round the ground floor, dated 1965, recording the history of the Old Kent Road from the arrival of the Romans, the Canterbury Pilgrims, the Jack Cade rebellion, the return of Charles II, to a local bobby and the Pearly King and Queen. It is the largest secular mural by Adam Kossowski (1905–86), a refugee from Soviet internment who worked for the Polish Ministry of Information in London before developing his distinctive ceramics with Fr Malachy Lynch at The Friars, Aylesford, Kent. Here the thick tiles combine raised, highly glazed, detailed and decorative sections against darker backgrounds. The building was approved for demolition in 2019, with the murals set to be relocated in the replacement housing and church.

CENTRAL CLINIC

Orchard Street, Swansea

1966–69; H. T. Wykes, Borough Architect; Harry Everington, sculptor

Herbert Tom Wykes was the borough architect between 1946 and 1966, responsible for many of Swansea's housing estates and schools. One of his last works was an office block for Swansea's housing and children's department, including a central welfare clinic and caretaker's flat, designed in December 1964. The four-storey building epitomises functional modernism, with a main glazed façade and brick end walls.

The building's special interest is the sculptural relief at the entrance by Harry Everington (1929–2000), briefly head of fine art at Swansea Art College in the 1960s, after studying at Leeds College of Art and the Slade. He went on to found the Frink School of Figurative Sculpture in Staffordshire in 1996, but here his figures are profoundly abstracted, a queue of people poised, about to burst into life as health and hope are restored. The commission befitted the description of him in his obituary as 'an enthusiastic, determined man with an indomitable spirit, [who] spent much of his career at odds with those whom he dubbed "grey men" – anyone in a suit who sought to interfere with his art of teaching'. The relief was cleaned by Catrin Saran James and a team of volunteers in 2017, which they called an act of 'reverse vandalism' to raise the relief's profile. In 2021 a new welfare centre is set to be built here, making the Central Clinic yet another building to be demolished in Swansea's once homogeneous post-war city centre, and putting the future of the relief in doubt.

FORMER INTERNATIONAL WOOL SECRETARIAT

Ilkley, West Yorkshire
1968; Richard Collick
William Mitchell mural listed grade II

The International Wool Secretariat was founded in 1937 by the woolgrowers of Australia, New Zealand and South Africa, and developed into a worldwide organisation after 1945. It opened a new technical centre in Valley Drive on the edge of Ilkley, convenient for the British wool industry centred on Leeds and Bradford but an unlikely sight in a street of suburban detached houses. The design by Richard Collick of local firm Chippendale & Edmondson was a simple grid of lightweight concrete offices, save for its central feature of a large, fan-shaped, first-floor lecture theatre which projects over the entrance like an over-scaled canopy. The International Wool Secretariat moved out of the building in the late 1990s and it is now used as private offices by a number of small local companies.

Collick brought in Bill Mitchell (1925–2020) to produce a suitable mural for the prominent curved end wall. His bold design depicts an abstracted flock of sheep with side panels representing manufacturing processes and the scientific analysis of wool. The panels were constructed of glass-reinforced polyester (GRP), using what was then a novel use of the material as the finished work rather than as a mould. He then coated them with polyester resin mixed with particles of bronze. Much cheaper than cast bronze, Mitchell had pioneered the technique the year before for the giant doors of Liverpool Cathedral, one of the works of which he was most proud. He went on to use GRP and resins more extensively in his later classical work.

APOLLO PAVILION

Oakerside Drive, Peterlee, County Durham
1969; Victor Pasmore
Listed grade II*

'An architecture and sculpture of purely abstract form through which to walk, in which to linger and on which to play,' wrote the artist Victor Pasmore (1908–98) of the two-storey sculptural bridge he created where a small stream tumbles into Blunts Dene. The idea of a lake at this point was made by Peterlee's general manager Vivian Williams, but Pasmore suggested it needed a 'dramatic emphasis'. He had been appointed in 1956 to give a fresh eye to the relationship between architecture and landscape, becoming responsible for the housing layouts and choice of materials.

The model for the pavilion closely resembles the wooden relief sculptures which Pasmore designed from around 1950, having embraced abstraction two years earlier. He wanted the sculpture to share the cubic quality of the nearby houses but expressed in reinforced concrete and cantilevers rather than brickwork. The result is a giant climbing frame, distorted by amoebic shapes in black paint. Its completion in 1969 coincided with the Apollo 11 moon launch, hence Pasmore's preferred name for his creation, though it is commonly referred to as the Pasmore Pavilion. He and his son John designed other smaller sculptures for Peterlee, including one for the town centre now also at Blunts Dene, and one set between the nearby pub and shop. Much of the nearby housing was poorly built, and residents sought retribution in the 1990s by wanting to demolish the pavilion. Instead a restoration programme was brilliantly promoted by a local student, Brian Sherriff, and completed in 2007.

HENGE

Beaufort Drive, Glenrothes
1970; David Harding
Listed grade C

Henge is 13 concrete slabs in a spiral formation, which rise in height to 9ft (2.75m). Their inside faces reference Pictish and Celtic symbols, or heroes of the 1960s including the Beatles, Bob Dylan, Che Guevara, Pelé, Martin Luther King and Dylan Thomas. The largest quotes Gandhi: 'Man's best monument is not a thing of stone but consists in living deeds ...' A cobbled seat in the centre offers contemplation in semi-concealment. *Henge* was a response to the Neolithic stone circle at nearby Balbirnie that was discovered in 1950 and relocated in 1970, but it uses the same concrete as the surrounding housing. Harding had no budget for special materials.

In 1968 the Glenrothes Development Corporation advertised for an artist to collaborate with its architects and engineers to give the town an identity, the new colliery having failed. Unlike Victor Pasmore at Peterlee, whose role was as a landscape adviser, David Harding (1937–) lived in the town and had a studio in the corporation workshops where he produced art in collaboration with the corporation's builders and often with schoolchildren. Concrete mushrooms sprout, hippopotami (by apprentice Stanley Bonnar) graze on traffic islands and, in the town park, pathways incorporate short poems, concrete columns trace the history of Western art and a pedestrian underpass recalls local industries. Harding went on to establish the Environmental Art Department at Glasgow School of Art in 1985, but he considers *Henge* to be one of his most important projects.

'GREAT WALL'

The Ringway (A451), Kidderminster
1972–73; William Mitchell
Listed grade II

Like most industrial towns in the 1960s, Kidderminster looked to relieve its compact centre from traffic congestion. Jack G. Stewart, borough engineer and surveyor, duly designed a ring road, which was built in four phases between 1965 and 1983. The third stretch, set east of the town below Comberton Hill, required a 1,050ft (320m) retaining wall against the hillside, a concrete cliff over 20ft (6.1m) at its highest point. The borough decided at an early stage on a decorative finish to soften its visual impact, and the local contractors, George Law & Co., attended a seminar at the Cement and Concrete Association that reported on Mitchell's sculpted wall for a flyover at Gateshead. Bill Mitchell was first appointed by the London County Council in 1957 to decorate its housing estates and traffic underpasses using materials from its building sites and, in his extensive independent practice, was among the first to exploit the possibilities of decorating large-scale pieces of traffic engineering. He was proud of the Kidderminster wall for its epic scale and integration with landscaping by Douglas H. Smith.

Mitchell produced a series of concrete panels with a deeply profiled surface finish cast using polystyrene liners to suggest a rugged natural rock face, into which he inserted ten more individually textured sections produced with more detailed fibreglass moulds. He also created a waterfall close to Comberton Hill roundabout, where there is the greatest pedestrian footfall, which was restored in 2021 following local fundraising as a Covid memorial.

CULTURE AND SPORT

OLD VIC
THEATRE ANNEX

The Cut, Lambeth, London
1957–58; Lyons Israel Ellis
Listed grade II

The Annex was one of central London's first brutalist buildings, a fittingly industrial aesthetic for the wardrobe, props and scenery departments to the Old Vic theatre next door. It is a rough, tough building, expected to take hard knocks, but also a model for the South Bank. The Old Vic, built in 1818, had a heady history in the 20th century, when Lilian Baylis took over from her aunt Emma Cons and brought Shakespeare to a popular audience. The Old Vic Theatre Company, founded in 1929 and led by John Gielgud, was the forerunner of the National Theatre Company incorporated in 1962. North American tours and the sale of its old workshops in Hampstead funded The Annex. Lawrence Israel devised the plan, as was customary for the practice, but the elevations by Tom Ellis and John Miller marked a new rigour and architectural quality for a firm where many young architects got their first jobs. The building expressed its functions in honest board-marked concrete, and a slot between its frontage block and rear loading dock, now glazed, denotes the position of a vertical paint frame set in a three-storey void through the building for painting scenery. The slot allowed the completed canvases to be hoisted out of the building and carried to the theatre across the road.

Since 1984 the building has been used as a theatre 'laboratory', with studios and writers' workshops. It was refurbished as studios for the Royal National Theatre in 2007 by Haworth Tompkins.

ELEPHANT AND RHINO HOUSE

London Zoo, Regent's Park, London
1962–65; Casson & Conder
Listed grade II*

Hugh Casson and Neville Conder had produced a plan for London Zoo in 1958, which led to a major rebuilding programme. Many of the new buildings were produced by the in-house architect Franz Stengelhofen, but the firm designed a bridge, and replaced Anthony Salvin's Elephant and Rhino House of the 1860s. This was supposed to be Casson's job, but in practice Conder and their assistants undertook the detailed design. They likened the grouping of cubicles, set in pairs for four elephants and four rhinos, to the animals themselves drinking at a pool. Copper-clad light scoops in the roof were a common feature of Conder's work, while he gave his source for the hacked-back corduroy concrete as Twickenham Bridge of 1928–33 – chosen because the elephants could rub against it without causing damage and already used by him at Cambridge. The Zoological Society had realised in the 1930s that architecture could create an appealing setting and could reflect the animals' characters as well as provide for their needs. Conder's building is a more complex development of Lubetkin and Tecton's design for an elephant house at Whipsnade Zoo based on the animals' turning circles.

Inside the roof scoops directed natural light on the animals, while humans were corralled into the enclosure's centre and kept in the gloom. However, the building, now known as the Casson Pavilion, is closed to the public; the elephants and rhinos moved many years ago to more spacious accommodation at Whipsnade.

GALA FAIRYDEAN ROVERS STAND

Netherdale, Galashiels
1963–64; Peter Womersley
Listed grade A

Gala Fairydean had a fine football team in the early 1960s, a string of local cup successes leading in 1966 to a sadly unsuccessful application to join the Scottish Football League. Meanwhile, a local lottery raised £25,000 to improve the ground with a new stand, opened with a special match in November 1964 against league side East Fife. The stand seated 620 spectators above changing rooms, showers, a kitchen and clubroom (since extended).

Womersley had designed a sports building at Hull University and was beginning to explore the artistry of board-marked concrete. The Netherdale stand is built to a 5in (12.7cm) module based on the Douglas fir boarding used for the formwork and expressed in the final finish. Engineered by Ove Arup & Partners, the canopy cantilevers 15ft (4.6m) either side of the end piers and 26ft (7.9m) forward over the spectators. The diagonal upstand beams of the canopy leave the soffit free for four floodlights. All this is realised as a series of triangular shapes, without obstructive piers facing the pitch and expressed as a backbend to the road where ground-floor brickwork is topped by clerestory glazing to show it is simply infill. Most striking are the inverse pyramids or umbrellas – counter three-dimensional triangles on single supports over twin turnstiles to either side, giving separate entrances to the ground and stand.

Gala Fairydean Rovers were first formed in 1894, split in two, then reunited in 2013. The club are proud of their unique stand, which is undergoing restoration by David Narro Associates.

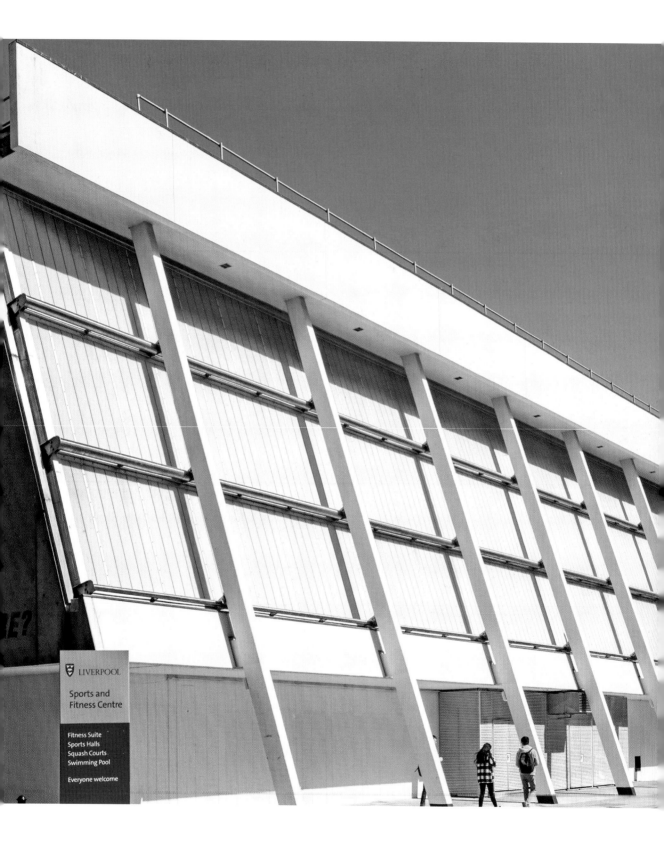

UNIVERSITY SPORTS CENTRE

Bedford Street North, Liverpool
1963–66; Denys Lasdun & Partners

This is the most startling and assertive, not only of Liverpool University's post-war buildings, as claimed by Nikolaus Pevsner, but of Denys Lasdun's whole indomitable oeuvre. Lasdun objected to Pevsner's description, claiming no intentional affront to its neighbours. Nevertheless, the way the frontage thrusts towards its late Georgian neighbours remains shocking. Part of this vigour came from the building's cradle-like form, front and back, until it was extended to the rear by Austin-Smith:Lord in 2003–05.

This vigorous appearance comes from external supports of raked, pre-stressed, precast columns, which transfer the relatively high wind-loading on the façade through the roof structure to the core and foundations. They allow the 108ft (33m) swimming pool behind to be entirely glazed on the street elevation, with precast slabs to the end. The original symmetry expressed the building's purpose, for on the other side a sports hall was similarly glazed, until the addition was made. This was originally the most interesting part of the building, for dry sports centres were a new building type in the 1960s, the universities at the forefront of their development thanks to government money intended for examination halls. The climbing wall at one end resembles an abstract sculpture; designed by Lasdun's associate Donald Norman Mill, it claimed to be the first in the country. By the mid-1960s, Lasdun was chiefly occupied by vast commissions such as the University of East Anglia and National Theatre (see pages 102 and 220), so this relatively modest (but not cheap) building has additional interest.

QUEEN ELIZABETH HALL AND HAYWARD GALLERY

Belvedere Road, London

1963–68; London County Council; team leader Norman Engleback

The Royal Festival Hall was to have included a smaller auditorium, but site problems led the LCC to design a hall on adjoining land, to which was added a gallery for touring exhibitions. Leslie Martin, chief architect, passed the job to a special group led by Norman Engleback. They treated the design as separate components so as not to compete with the bulk of the Festival Hall nor disturb views from its terraces. A walkway had existed along the South Bank since 1951, which a new scheme in December 1957 replaced by a great platform across the site to cover car parking and linking the buildings at mid-level. It reflected the interactive town planning then appearing in the LCC's new town project at Hook or entries to the Hauptstadt competition for central Berlin; Ron Herron, Warren Chalk and Dennis Crompton, later members of Archigram, worked on details of the design. Engleback took the form of the QEH from the Zurich Tonhalle, adding the Purcell Room to the design in 1960.

The architects chose heavy concrete to repel external noise, particularly from helicopter services, though as built, precast panels lined the exterior rather than shuttered concrete. Since they were to be seen from above, roofs and ducts were detailed with equal care. The close-boarded concrete contrasted with white Macedonian marble and with doors, windows and bars in rough-cast anodised aluminium; for most projects the cost of such finishes would have been prohibitive. Henry Moore demanded natural light in the Hayward Gallery, first planned as a spiral of five galleries that could be used separately if required.

BARBICAN

City of London
1963–82; Chamberlin, Powell & Bon
Listed grade II

CP&B were already designing the Golden Lane Estate for the City corporation when they turned to the acres of bomb-damaged land between it and St Paul's Cathedral. Whereas Golden Lane epitomised mid-century modern, the Barbican is thoroughly brutalist in its pick-hammered concrete, the mighty chunks of aggregate appropriate to the complex's scale. Together they trace the development of mass housing in post-war Britain. A New Barbican Committee had proposed flats as an alternative to more offices in the City, and following its rejection in 1955 Peter (Joe) Chamberlin produced his own scheme. This combined flats and shops with the Guildhall School of Music and Drama, whose facilities were to double as a modest arts centre. A second scheme, in 1956, introduced the City of London School for Girls. The plan assumed its present appearance in 1959, though it was only in 1960 that a covered bridge was eliminated from the site and in 1961 the three towers assumed their triangular shape with upswept balconies to reduce wind resistance. When built they were the tallest residential towers in Europe.

In 1964 the City decided that a larger concert hall would be more viable. The insertion of a 2,000-seat concert hall and 1,500-seat theatre into a scheme already under construction explains the congested plan. The Pit and a conference centre were added only shortly before construction began in 1972. By the time the arts centre opened, the Falklands War was looming and its lavish public provision seemed out of time.

DOLLAN AQUA CENTRE

Brouster Hill, East Kilbride
1964–68; Alexander Buchanan Campbell
Listed grade A

With so many young people but little funding, the new towns were desperate for community and sports facilities. The government placed the onus on local authorities to make the provision, but few were able or willing; a rare exception was Fifth District Council and its successor the East Kilbride Burgh, formed in 1963. The earliest drawings by Alexander Buchanan Campbell (1914–2007) show a very tall, rectangular building using laminated timber beams, before first an asymmetrical vault was preferred, and then the realised scheme of long narrow vaults supported on four giant trusses approved in 1963. The result is a theatrical and emphatic reinforced-concrete structure, internally four shell vaults each made of small vaulted sections and supported externally by giant vaults, where each rib splays out to form two colossal diagonal struts. Even they are dominated by the giant chimney stack. Campbell's sources were Pier Luigi Nervi's Palazzetto dello Sport, built in 1957 ahead of the Rome Olympics, and then Kenzo Tange's gymnasia for the 1964 Tokyo Olympics, which he saw under construction. Scotland's first competition-length swimming pool, the interior and east elevation were modernised in 1995 by Faulkner Brown and repaired again in 2008–11, but the west elevation remains daring and uncompromising. It fits its parkland setting superbly. Campbell had served articles with Gillespie, Kidd & Coia before joining the Glasgow Office of Public Works; he went on to design the adjoining youth centre in 1966–70 but this is much his finest work.

BILLINGHAM FORUM

Billingham, County Durham
1965–67; Alan J. Ward of Elder & Lester
Theatre listed grade II

Billingham was made prosperous by Imperial Chemical Industries, which in 1926 took over a wartime fertiliser factory subsequently expanded with the discovery of anhydrite. Their business rates supported the building of a new town centre, over a mile from the old high street, which included a pedestrian shopping arcade, flats, a library and the La Ronde nightclub and casino. To this the borough added a combined sports centre and theatre, spending its capital resources ahead of absorption into the new county of Teesside in 1968. The Queen opened the unique complex in October 1967, commemorated by Bainbridge Copnall's oversize sculpture of a family group symbolic of the borough's concept for the town.

The Forum has four elements linked by foyers: a swimming pool, ice rink, indoor sports centre and theatre. The first three are built of local steel, the ice rink roof supported on rope trusses hung between arches that are supported on raked columns held apart at their base by compression beams. Only the theatre is built of brick and concrete, for sound insulation, and is novel in its horseshoe plan with three tiers of boxes – based on Italian opera houses and again planned for a family group on a night out. The centre was drastically remodelled in 2011, when even the listed theatre was reclad in yellow and blue tiles; only the ice rink retains its dramatic elevations. The foyers had already lost their mosaic interiors. Yet the ambition of the town centre remains palpable.

MERTON COLLEGE SPORTS PAVILION

Manor Road, Oxford
1966; Michael G. D. Dixey
Listed grade II

This is a simple building, just a club room and bar, with changing rooms on one side and a groundsman's flat on the other, and a block of four squash courts in a linked wing to the rear. It sits in a big landscape where Oxford opens out to the river, its suburbs delicately screened from sight by the landscape architects Richard Sudell & Partners, who specialised in sports grounds. Dixey came to specialise in recreation buildings, but he had earlier visited Le Corbusier's state capital buildings in Chandigarh, India.

The one set of nearby buildings are equally significant representatives of a different genre: the long residential ranges of St Catherine's College, the original part by Arne Jacobsen. Having sold upstart St Catherine's its tight site by the river, Merton College had to assert its ancient mastery on the remaining ground with a building that respected its famous neighbour but on its own terms and at moderate cost. Though a far smaller building, it stands out through the quality and greater boldness of its materials – board-marked concrete with dark brick infill, set back on the ground floor, and for the squash courts. The double-height club room is almost completely glazed, as is the first-floor link to the squash courts. A thick timber balustrade to the first-floor balcony enforces the strong horizontal rhythm. The interior is equally tough in its materials, with bare brick walls, paviours and quarry tiles for the floors to withstand spiked boots, and timber slatted ceilings.

NEW CLUB

84–87 Princes Street, Edinburgh
1966–69; Alain Reiach of Reiach and Hall
Listed grade A

The New Club is one of Scotland's oldest and most distinguished clubs, built on this site in 1834 by William Burn, extended by David Bryce and later remodelled by Robert Lorimer. By 1964 it wanted more facilities, including an annexe for female members (full membership not being extended to women until 2010!) and a swimming pool.

Patrick Abercrombie and Derek Plumstead's master plan for Edinburgh in 1949 drew attention to the city's congestion, leading in 1954 to the appointment of the 'Princes Street Panel' of architects. Their solution, evolved from 1958 but published only in 1967, was to slowly redevelop the hodgepodge of commercial properties with a first-floor promenade. These would eventually link up as a second shopping street – and would have been one of Britain's most prominent brutalist megastructures. However, only seven properties were rebuilt before the policy was abandoned in 1982, of which the New Club is the most distinguished. It is clad in Aberdeenshire granite on the Princes Street façade, with stepped-out mullions and elsewhere a combination of aggregate panels and grey brickwork. The entrance is modestly concealed between shops, with parking tucked into the steep slope behind. After this pinch the three-storey, top-lit central hall appears larger and still more striking, its staircase balustrade finished in coloured tesserae to contrast with the dark brick walls. The interconnected sitting rooms overlook the fabulous views towards the Old Town, their scale and bold details suited to the furniture and fittings brought from the old club, including panelling by Lorimer in the dining room at the rear.

ULSTER MUSEUM EXTENSION

Botanic Gardens, Belfast
1966–70; Francis Pym and John F. Harrison,
Government of Northern Ireland
Listed grade B+

One of the first signs of the 21st-century brutalist revival was the controversy in 2007 aroused by the remodelling of Pym's additions to the Ulster Museum. The old museum by James Cumming Wynnes had been delayed by the First World War and abandoned when less than half was completed; its extension and a renaming were intended to make it the leading museum in Northern Ireland. A competition was held in 1963, a last moment of optimism for the province, assessed by Leslie Martin. Pym's winning design countered the verticality of the old classical columns with sweeping bands of concrete in a series of projecting and receding forms like a set of cupboard drawers, low at the bottom for displays of local and natural history, rising to tall spaces with rooflights for the picture gallery at the top. Banding in the concrete forges links with the rustication of the classical stonework. Pym resigned his contract in 1968 to become an Anglican priest and the building was completed by the architect's department at the province's finance ministry, but in 1971 *Building Design* declared it the best museum in the British Isles. It was also Pym's only major building.

The arguments in 2007 centred on the loss of a series of internal ramps, reminiscent of the processional routes within Le Corbusier's family of galleries at Ahmedabad, Chandigarh and Tokyo, and of the concrete finishes. These all duly disappeared, as did a glass wall under the curved entrance canopy.

ROYAL NATIONAL THEATRE

Upper Ground, Lambeth, London
1969–76; Denys Lasdun & Partners
Listed grade II*

One of Britain's finest and most popular brutalist buildings, the National Theatre sits splendidly on its promontory site overlooking the Thames, its views orchestrated as though the City was itself a stage set. The idea of a national theatre originated in 1847, and its sponsors laid a foundation stone in Kensington before securing a site on the South Bank from the London County Council in 1942. Lasdun won a competition in 1963 for a theatre and opera house near County Hall, chosen because he offered fresh solutions based on pure space to the committee's often contradictory brief. When the opera part was dropped, he made a new scheme for the theatre's final site.

The building takes its form from the two main auditoria, set at 45 degrees to each other and denoted by a structural grid aligned on the largest, the Olivier Theatre. This fixes the fly towers and main stairs and is seen in the foyer's coffering, most dramatically where turned through 45 degrees in the half serving the Lyttelton Theatre. It is unusual for the largest theatre in a complex to be the most innovative, but when Lasdun was making his designs the National Theatre Company had access to the traditional Old Vic nearby (see page 198). Lasdun could then devote himself to creating the innovative Olivier, with its corner apron stage and side slips. A studio space, originally the Cottesloe Theatre but since 2014 known as the Dorfman Theatre, was designed by theatre specialist Iain Mackintosh.

EAST STAND,
ST JAMES' PARK

Newcastle upon Tyne

1970–73; John Farthing of Faulkner-Brown, Hendy, Watkinson & Stonor

Newcastle United plays its football in the heart of the city, each adding vitality to the other on match days. Two local clubs amalgamated in 1892 and built a ground on the Town Moor, which became St James' Park. After promotion back to the top division in 1965, United looked to expand the ground. An initial joint venture with the city council and university in 1968 failed to stack up financially, but the club won the European Fairs Cup in 1969 and reached the quarter-finals the following year, fuelling renewed optimism. Building began in 1972 with the East Stand. But rising inflation, strike action and relegation ensured no more was built.

Part of the cost was due to the need to respect the adjacent listed Leazes Terrace, Thomas Oliver's masterpiece. Subsequent demolition of smaller neighbours has left the two structures in a direct stand-off. They could not be more different, despite a considered similarity in height. Faulkner-Brown chose a ribbed concrete finish, which they then chipped to reveal an aggregate of warm, local stone, creating a curious harmony. The structure itself is a tall, exposed cantilever, braced by a rear channel beam, the seating slab and front wall, with steel trusses supporting the aluminium roof and floodlights. The practice came to specialise in libraries and sports buildings – an odd pairing of which this is their largest venture, with Harry Faulkner-Brown personally designing 50ft (15m) lettering for the main frontage, now gone. The Royal Fine Art Commission rejected further rebuilding proposals in 2008.

ASSEMBLY ROOMS

Market Place, Derby
1971–77; Casson & Conder

The architectural critic Ian Nairn in 1961 admired Derby's Market Place for its vitality, but in 1963 the elegant 18th-century assembly hall burned down. The market stalls were dispatched to a new shopping centre, the north side of the square was demolished and amid the wreckage a limited competition was held in 1969–70 for new civic halls. The brief asked the architects to retain the old façade, but this was eventually rebuilt at Crich Tramway Museum; James Stirling's scheme retaining it at a 40-degree angle is better known than Neville Conder's final building.

The scheme is a refinement of earlier halls by Conder at Cambridge University. The palette of zinc mansard roofs, dark brick and concrete mullions is similar, but there is an exceptional refinement in the concrete of the exposed slabs. The large hall is rectangular with a balcony, designed for concerts, theatre, banquets and sports events, with a stage dropped down or a dumb waiter that can be raised as required. An early concert programme began with AC/DC but virtually ended in 1982. A glazed promenade across the front over ground-floor shops links it when required to the smaller hall seating 500 and to a projecting VIP suite. A covered arcade for market stalls was never used but provides shelter and a sculptural contrast of light and shade to the main elevation.

The building was due to be refurbished after a fire in the rear car park in 2014. Yet although the halls survive undisturbed, in 2021 councillors voted for demolition.

CHILDREN'S SLIDE

Brunel Estate, Westbourne Park Road, London
1973–74; Michael Brown
Listed grade II

An exhibition at the RIBA in 2015 drew attention to the 'brutalist playground', the innovative slides and climbing equipment introduced on urban estates in the post-war years. It was at odds with the contemporary growth of adventure playgrounds, where children were encouraged to make their own climbing structures and dens. Advances in earth moulding and the arrival of impact-absorbing cushioned surfaces in the early 1970s made possible more adventurous fixed slides. Ernö Goldfinger made a feature of play structures on his estates, and the remains of that at Balfron Tower disappeared only in 2019; the serpentine slides created by Mary Mitchell as part of her landscape projects in northern England disappeared several years ago. That has left the slide at the Brunel Estate as the great survivor.

Westminster City Council built a new estate on Mileage Yard, derelict railway sidings, in 1970–74 to the designs of Frank G. West, formerly of the London County Council. For the landscaping between the big slabs he brought in Michael Brown, who had studied landscape design in the United States and worked with Eric Lyons before setting up his own practice specialising in housing estates. He first planned his modified contours using a sandpit in the office, and the sloping brick embankments that protect the landscaping at the Brunel Estate became a trademark. The brick slide structure remains, though footholds, step-irons and hand-hold posts that encouraged children to climb the brickwork have gone; instead, more handrails have imposed new hazards.

THEATR CLWYD

Raikes Lane, Mold, Flintshire
1973–76; Robert W. Harvey, county architect
Listed grade II

When in 1969 Flintshire County Council proposed to build an arts centre, its councillors promised 'a powerhouse for cultural activities', with two theatres, a ballroom, cinema, television studio and restaurant. Theatr Clwyd was the most northerly of a network of theatres built across Wales, also including Harlech and Swansea, and – with its own resident repertory company – perhaps the most ambitious. The main hall for 550 people adopts the crescent plan and rough walling made fashionable by Rod Ham's Thorndike Theatre at Leatherhead, opened in 1969, while the small studio was modelled on Edward Mendelsohn's Cockpit Theatre in London. The assemblage of spaces tumbles gracefully down the steep hillside, meeting at the bottom in a double-height entrance hall fronted in glass and lead, lead copings elsewhere contrasting with the bold red brickwork of the remainder. The underlying steel frame may be a homage to the area's traditional industries.

Theatr Clwyd was also the last of a group of stunning civic buildings by Harvey for Flintshire County Council, gathered on the Llwynegrin estate above the tiny town. These began in 1966–68 with the Shire Hall, rhythmically patterned in black and white panels owing something to Eero Saarinen's American Embassy, followed by law courts and a library in 1969. The lower ranges of the Shire Hall were demolished in 2020 for housing, and of all Harvey's notable brutalist buildings only Theatr Clwyd is listed and likely to survive. However, alterations to the frontage were proposed by Haworth Tompkins in 2021.

THEATR ARDUDWY

Coleg Harlech, St David's Hill, Harlech
1973–78; Gerald Latter of Colwyn Foulkes & Partners
Listed grade II*

Coleg Harlech was the 'college of the second chance', a residential centre for
mature students founded in 1927 out of the Workers' Education Association. Thomas
Jones, private secretary to Lloyd George, secured Plas Wernfawr, a house by the
Arts and Crafts architect George Walton, to which Griffith Morris added a library
in 1938. In 1965 Thomas Jeffreys-Jones restructured the academic programme,
introducing a two-year diploma course for students that was the college's greatest
achievement. Ralph Colwyn Foulkes built an 11-storey tower (linked to the hillside
at its sixth-floor level) with 100 study bedrooms in 1968, only for Plas Wernfawr's
great hall to burn down the same year. In its stead, Latter designed a 260-seat
theatre that doubled as a community arts centre that presented a mixture of local
and professional drama productions as well as film shows.

    The theatre's aesthetic is as tough as that of the castle sitting on the nearby crag
that dominates the coast, and it is similarly vertiginous. Its stepped auditorium, an
inverted cone, rises behind a concrete frame above a glazed foyer and offices, with
projecting staircases treated separately. The interior, by contrast, is vibrantly colourful
down to its terrazzo tiles. Coleg Harlech closed in 2017 and the site sold on twice
with vain promises so far that the theatre will reopen, though work is going on.
However, the future for the totally derelict residential tower seems bleak.

THE ELEPHANT SPORTS CENTRE

Cox Street/Pool Meadow, Coventry
1974–76; Harry Noble, city architect

The Elephant is the product of a singular circumstance: a pre-existing pool of high quality (now listed), a unique site over Cox Street to be spanned on four legs, and a local authority with architectural ambition. The shape evolved accordingly, and an elephant appears on the city's coat of arms as well as the city standard of 1949. The dry sports centre shared catering and sauna facilities with its elegant neighbour but is otherwise entirely different – dark instead of light, humped instead of smooth.

Above ground-floor workshops and disabled parking rise five storeys of accommodation, including a bowling green, squash courts and a practice area for sports ranging from rifle shooting to table tennis. At the top is a three-storey hall for football, fencing and boxing. The structure is precast concrete faced in profiled aluminium sheeting, with a tubular sheet steel roof that incorporated specialised lighting for boxing, and bronzed patent glazing.

In 1960 the Wolfenden Report revealed a shortage of sports halls, and the Albemarle Report for the Central Council for Physical Recreation recommended more be built for teenagers. Coventry's combination of two contrasting buildings is unique. As part of Coventry's term as UK City of Culture, the words of local author George Eliot, 'It is always fatal to have music or poetry interrupted,' were projected on to the building in May 2021. It had closed in 2020 and was threatened with demolition until a petition was launched to save it. It has now been put up for rent.

RECREATION CENTRE

Brixton Station Road, Brixton, London
1974–83; George Finch, Lambeth Architect's Department
Listed grade II

Ted Hollamby, Lambeth's chief architect, conceived a recreation centre as the hub of a new high-level town centre, planned in connection with two motorways as set out in the Greater London Development Plan of 1969. He commissioned a design from one of his leading design groups, led by Finch, previously a housing specialist. Built over six levels, the top floor featured two swimming pools with stunning views across London, above a sports hall, bowls hall, squash courts, a gymnasium and facilities for judo, shooting and cricket. It also had a restaurant, bar, cafés and a dance space. Provision for so many activities in one building was still novel save at Billingham (see page 212) and the younger universities, visited by Finch. He wanted the interior spaces to be interconnected and welcoming, so that all visitors to the building could experience the bustle and activity, so finding inspiration to participate. All the facilities are reached from a full-height atrium, with a climbing wall on one side, so spectators can follow an assent from the safety of the stairs.

A hub of Brixton's black community, a plaque commemorates the visit of Nelson Mandela in 1996. Shops line Brixton Station Road and an office block, International House, rises from the north-east corner of the site. Their red brick is that found in the commercial buildings of the surrounding streets, though this is overshadowed by the massive concrete structure which also supports a walkway that is the only part of the elevated town centre to survive.

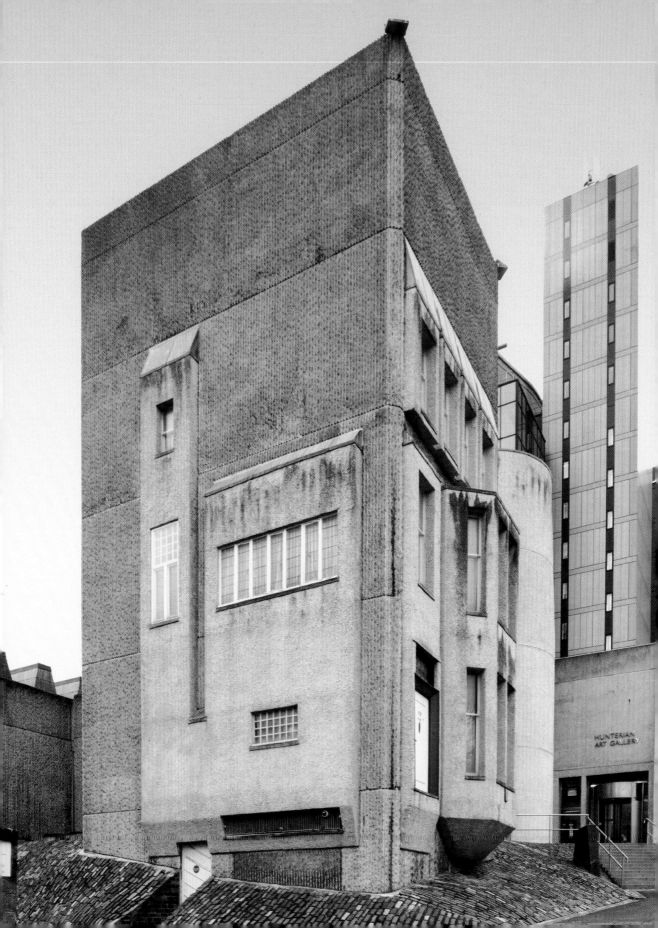

HUNTERIAN ART GALLERY AND MACKINTOSH HOUSE

Glasgow
1975–81; William Whitfield

Brutalism meets Mackintosh. Whitfield's new art gallery includes a recreation of the interior layout, decoration and furnishing of No.78 Southpark Avenue, Charles Rennie Mackintosh's home from 1906–1914, demolished by the University of Glasgow as part of its expansion. Whitfield was first commissioned to design a new library in 1961, just as he was undertaking major works at Durham and Newcastle universities. An 11-storey complex built in 1966–68 with service towers strongly reminiscent of Louis Kahn's medical research towers at the University of Philadelphia, it has been overclad in bland grey panels and pale stone that try to disarm its dramatic shape. What survives beautifully is the extension for the university's art collection. The top-lit picture galleries, opened in 1978, are kept low-key to allow the collections to speak for themselves, so fireworks passed to the staircase and Eduardo Paolozzi's monumental cast-aluminium doors.

Thoughts of preserving Mackintosh's house began in the 1940s, and when the university resolved on demolition in 1963 it agreed to recreate the house. Whitfield himself visited No.78 in 1961, and every fitting and scrap of joinery was preserved. In 1964 the curator Andrew McLaren Young set out proposals for a thorough reconstruction, for which Whitfield produced plans in 1970–71. The abiding image is of Mackintosh's rendered bay frontage and strip windows shining out between heavy corduroy concrete – Whitfield's concrete nap is most forceful – and a front door suspended in mid-air has the fossilised quality of a Rachel Whiteread sculpture.

PLACES OF WORSHIP

ST PAUL

Burdett Road, Bow Common, London
1958–60; Robert Maguire and Keith Murray
Listed grade II*

St Paul's stark, geometric box of brick and concrete signifies its importance not
only architecturally, but as an expression of the Liturgical Movement's arrival in the
Church of England. It was the personal vision of the anarchical socialist Fr Gresham
Kirkby, appointed to the bombed-out Victorian church in 1951 and who stayed
until 1994. He admired the clean light of Thaxted parish church, and a freestanding
altar installed at the nearby Royal Foundation of St Katharine by the silversmith Keith
Murray, who introduced him to Maguire. They formed a partnership and founded
the New Churches Research Group, which embraced the ideas of Peter Hammond,
a campaigner for the expression of a closer relationship between celebrant and
congregation who featured St Paul's in his ground-breaking book, *Liturgy and
Architecture* (1960).

Maguire brought to St Paul's the interest in natural materials honestly expressed
and the classical logic of Renaissance church building expounded by Rudolf
Wittkower, which had so influenced the Smithsons. St Paul's is a stepped cube based
around a central altar set under a glazed pyramidal roof. It is raised up two steps
beneath a ciborium of black steel. The congregation sit on four sides on benches,
and around them runs a processional route behind a segmental arched arcade, later
decorated with mosaics by Charles Lutyens. There are projecting side chapels and
an entrance porch, where – symbolically – sits the font, formed from an off-the-peg
industrial vat. The porch itself features lettering by Ralph Beyer, then also working at
Coventry Cathedral.

241

ST BRIDE

Whitemoss Avenue, East Kilbride
1959–63; Metzstein and MacMillan of Gillespie, Kidd & Coia
Listed grade A

St Bride's was GKC's largest church and perhaps the most remarkable church in any new town. This is despite the demolition in 1983 of a freestanding 90ft (27.4m) campanile that stood at the crest of the steep path rising from Whitemoss Avenue. The church stands symbolically on a high bank between the old and new parts of the town. The rectangular single-volume interior, made asymmetrical by a freestanding gallery on its long north side, has a forward altar but is otherwise traditional in plan. The asymmetry and, in particular, the south wall punched randomly with fenestration is indebted ultimately to Le Corbusier's Notre Dame du Haut at Ronchamp, but on a massively increased scale to seat 800 worshippers. Structurally, the building is a mass of load-bearing brickwork that works as a total piece of sculpture. The brick provides the detailing internally, with exposed concrete beams and the altar, font and stoups made of granite. Externally, the roughness, curves and irregular patterning of the brickwork suggest Alvar Aalto, not least his weekend retreat at Muuratsalo in central Finland on a massively enlarged scale. His influence and that of Sigurd Leverenz also inform the copper-roofed office and presbytery complex as well as the brick-paved courtyard that it encloses. Three copper-clad light funnels resembling that at Le Corbusier's La Tourette soar above exposed timber spars, so that natural light was diffused internally; water penetration led to these windows being blocked and artificial lighting now dominates, despite a careful restoration programme in 2016.

ST MARY

Broadfield Drive, Leyland, Lancashire
1962–64; Jerzy Faczynski of Weightman & Bullen
Listed grade II

Benedictine monks first built a church at Leyland in 1854. The tiny town expanded rapidly in the 1950s with overspill from Manchester and the development of Leyland Motors, and briefly became the core of a new town for central Lancashire. The parish priest, Fr Edmund FitzSimons, determined to build a lavish new church. Inspired by the latest liturgical thinking, a tour of French and Swiss churches in 1959 and advice from Mgr James Crichton, he produced an octagonal balsawood model which he presented to Faczynski, a Polish refugee architect trained at Liverpool. The folded plate roof incorporates clerestory glazing that gives the interior its chief illumination.

The boldness of the circular body and detached concrete belfry is matched by artworks outside and in, by national and local designers. The ceramic frieze of the Last Judgement above the entrance is by Adam Kossowski, who also created the rood depicting Christ the King over the altar. The stations of the cross set between the 'V'-shaped concrete pillars of the circular arcade is by the left-wing Liverpudlian artist Arthur Dooley; while the Roman soldiers appear anonymous and brutalised, other figures are realistic depictions of local workmen. The outer face of the ambulatory is a wall of *dalle de verre* by Patrick Reyntiens representing the creation, while smaller sculptures are by David John, Ian Stuart, and Charles and Mary Blakeman. Faczynski designed a tapestry. Curved timber benches on a slightly raked floor add to the sense of theatricality, and to the completeness of Fr FitzSimon's vision.

ST PETER'S SEMINARY

Kilmahew House, Cardross, Dumbarton
1962–66; Gillespie, Kidd & Coia
Listed grade A

Brutalism in ruination assumes the power of the sublime, nowhere more than at St Peter, Cardross, a monument as affecting as any medieval monastery and more important for being the only post-war seminary. Yet years of dereliction and vandalism have left it a concrete skeleton on the brink of final collapse, abandoned by the Catholic Church and Historic Environment Scotland with a last hope resting with a tiny charity, the Kilmahew Education Trust.

In the hands of assistants Isi Metzstein and Andy MacMillan, GKC reinvented itself from the late 1950s as Scotland's most progressive architectural practice, working mainly for the Catholic Church. St Peter's was built in the grounds of 19th-century Kilmahew House for training novitiates for the priesthood, just as numbers plummeted and the church remodelled its education programme, demanding that they live in the urban community. After serving briefly as a drug rehabilitation centre, the complex was abandoned in 1987 and Kilmahew House demolished in 1995. Other parts have since subsided, leaving only the bones of the main rectangular, stepped structure. Inside, the dramatic single space evolved from a dining area at one end into a chapel at the other, overlooked by rows of cells, their exquisite timber finishes long substituted by graffiti. The long horizontals are balanced by five tall silos containing side altars for training the novices; they nod to those at Le Corbusier's Notre Dame de la Tourette, though its four-square plan and traditional spaces are conventional by comparison with Cardross.

METROPOLITAN CATHEDRAL OF CHRIST THE KING

Mount Pleasant, Liverpool
1962–67; Frederick Gibberd
Listed grade II*

While most cathedrals reveal themselves slowly as you explore them, entering Liverpool's Roman Catholic Cathedral is to be struck by a single arresting image of a vast auditorium bathed in red and blue light. This is made possible by the concrete construction, a drum supported on flying buttresses raised on a raft over car parking and the crypt that was all that was built of Sir Edwin Lutyens's baroque design of 1933. The original mosaic finishes have been overclad because of water ingress. Archbishop Heenan held a competition in 1960 for the new design, and Gibberd's centralised plan followed his brief that the congregation be set close to the celebration of the Mass, though the architect stressed that it was above all an art form. Its glazed corona is symbolic of Christ's crown of thorns and reflects the cathedral's dedication, the competition assessors considering that 'it powerfully expresses the kingship of Christ, because the whole building is conceived as a crown'. The design beat 289 other entries and offers a counterpoise to Sir Giles Scott's traditional Anglican cathedral at the other end of Hope Street.

John Piper and Patrick Reyntiens designed the main glass, after Heenan had admired their work at Coventry, and Margaret Traherne that in the Lady Chapel. The stone belfry and bronze outer doors feature relief panels by William Mitchell, and the Chapel of the Blessed Sacrament opposite the main entrance, expressed separately and resembling a giant wedge of cheese, has a mural by Ceri Richards.

MORTONHALL CREMATORIUM

Howden Hall Road, Edinburgh
1963–67; Sir Basil Spence, Glover and Ferguson
Listed grade A

Mortonhall Crematorium is the last and most dramatic of Spence's religious
buildings, designed with Hardie Glover, Anthony Blee, William 'Norman' Hunter
and Archie Dewar in 1961–62. Most of these architects were based in Edinburgh
but came to the main London office at key points in the design. The complex is set on
the southern edge of Edinburgh, where dense woodland makes a dramatic contrast
to the unexpectedly spiky profile of its concrete planes. The crematorium, chapel
and waiting shelter are arranged as a loose triangle of freestanding structures in an
open hollow at the end of a long drive, and correspondence shows that Spence had
been studying Gunnar Asplund's crematorium at Stockholm's Woodland Cemetery,
though the buildings are very different externally. The interiors have more in common
in their neutrality, the surprisingly small interior at Mortonhall featuring neutral,
white-painted finishes with pews and a ceiling of light pine. The plan was angled
to make the most of the sunlight, particularly from the west. Here lies the drama, the
light making one last unexpected contrast, as the narrow windows – concealed as
you enter the building – send striking shafts of primary colours from the afternoon
sun straight down the nave, with further hidden top-lighting illuminating the
catafalque, testament to Spence's love of theatricality and exhibition design.
It takes ideas begun at the Chapel of Unity, the last element designed at Coventry
Cathedral, and the chapel at Sussex University to their powerful conclusion as one
of his truly great buildings.

CHURCH OF OUR LADY HELP OF CHRISTIANS

Worth Abbey, West Sussex
1964–89; Francis Pollen
Listed grade II*

Francis Pollen (1926–87) was inspired to become an architect by Sir Edwin Lutyens, who had built Lambay Castle for his grandparents and became a family friend. He never embraced simple modernism, but took his classical training straight into the massiveness of brutalism. The debt to the Renaissance ideas of humanism and proportion expounded by Rudolf Wittkower's *Architectural Principles in the Age of Humanism* was a key text of the brutalists and of the Liturgical Movement, and is as important to the church as Pollen's deep and personal Catholic faith.

Worth Abbey was founded by Benedictines in 1930 as a daughter house of Downside Abbey and similarly ran a boys' school. Pollen's first design, in 1956, was for a tall elliptical church with a central altar surrounded by an ambulatory and side chapels. The final design was a circular space under a shallow dome, lit by a clerestory and supported on fat, elemental columns. The altar is almost central, but has none of the directional problems found at Liverpool Cathedral since slices are taken from the circle by two subsidiary chapels and a monks' choir. The building, a concrete frame infilled in brick, was realised only in stages by John Lyles, the school woodwork teacher, who supervised an in-house team of builders after professional contractors felt unable to handle so much curved brickwork. The foundation stone was laid in 1968 and the church consecrated in 1978, with little decoration save that of the structure itself; the surrounding offices were completed more slowly.

CATHEDRAL CHURCH OF SS PETER AND PAUL

Clifton, Bristol
1969–73; Ronald Weeks of the Sir Percy Thomas Partnership
Listed grade II*

Built in a remarkably short time for just £600,000, the rough wigwam-like exterior is a remarkable landmark. It claims to be the first cathedral in the world to accord completely with the liturgical guidelines issued by the Vatican in November 1963. These sought to involve the congregation by permitting the Mass to be celebrated in modern languages and for the celebrant to face them.

Weeks placed the top-lit sanctuary to one side, facing a fan of seating so the celebrant can see everyone at once. The result is a hexagonal space, and hexagons and equilateral triangles became the basis of the wigwam design, including its decorative detailing. Reinforced concrete of the highest quality made the broad span possible; to ensure consistency over three years of construction every bag of Portland white cement mix was prepared by one member of the Laing team, selected for his expertise. The hierarchy of the internal spaces is marked by a rising ceiling height, from the low entrance and baptistry into the main worship space, subtly lit by rooflights and rising to the three-part thrusting spire, symbolic of the Trinity. Colour is limited to the entrance, where a wall of *dalle de verre* glass by Henry Haig leads to the baptistry and shields first views of the main space. There, William Mitchell carved the low-relief Stations of the Cross in wet concrete, with just 1 ½ hours to complete each one before it set. The Portland stone font is by Simon Verity.

OFFICES AND INDUSTRY

SLIMES THICKENER

Hafodyrynys Colliery, Crumlin, Gwent
1954–58; architect unknown

Following the nationalisation of Britain's coal industry, the pit sunk at Hafodyrynys in 1911–14 (superseding a short-lived pit of 1878–80) was chosen for massive expansion. It was linked underground with three others in a £5.5 million scheme begun in 1954. New colliery buildings followed a functional modern design with concrete frames and shell roofs, infilled in brick and glass, and boasted the latest equipment. This included a washery, considered an important symbol of greater post-war efficiency, which extracted coal dust from slurry and dried the remaining waste before tipping, processes that were rare before the 1950s. The slimes thickener at the washery was a simple circular building of reinforced concrete on short stilts with a band of glazing and a concrete shell roof shaped like a flying saucer. Its appearance is a little reminiscent of Peter Behrens's circular brick water tower and tar silos built as part of his Frankfurt gasworks of 1911–12.

Despite so much investment, the colliery failed and closed in 1966, save for the washery, which continued to serve the other collieries nearby. The site was cleared in 1985 except for the slimes thickener, which was retained at the request of Sir Richard Hanbury-Tenison of Pontypool Park Estate, to which the site reverted. He commissioned plans for its conversion to a restaurant but did not proceed with the venture. Instead its simple, futuristic shape and splendid isolation have made it an arresting site by the A472 and a respected local landmark.

TRAWSFYNYDD NUCLEAR POWER STATION

Trawsfynydd, Gwynedd
1959–63; Sir Basil Spence & Partners

Trawsfynydd was the only nuclear power station in the UK to be built inland. It was cooled by water from the man-made Llyn Trawsfynydd reservoir built in the 1920s for the hydro-electric Maentwrog power station and part of the sensitive Snowdonia National Park. The plant, with its twin Magnox reactors, became operational in 1965 at a cost of £103 million.

Spence was brought in during 1958 by a construction consortium, Atomic Power Constructions. His design grouped the accommodation in four buildings, separating the station's distinct functions, with two for the reactors, one for the turbine hall and an electricity substation. He arranged them compactly and linked them by covered walkways. The concrete reactor buildings, two great boxes 180ft (55m) high, still dominate the site. As at Sussex University, Spence collaborated with the landscape architect Sylvia Crowe, whose hand is very evident here. She concealed the car parking and the bittiest elements of the electricity generation, sinking them behind the dam of the lake and lush tree planting. Soil and rock removed during the excavations were used to soften the newly constructed areas and local stone in the aggregate gave some harmony between the buildings and their site.

Closed in 1991, work to completely decommission Trawsfynydd is expected to take nearly a hundred years. There are proposals to develop the site for small modular reactors and associated technologies on site as Cwmni Egino, while alongside there is an excellent visitor centre and café.

METRO CENTRAL HEIGHTS, FORMERLY ALEXANDER FLEMING HOUSE

Elephant and Castle, London
1959–66; Ernö Goldfinger
Listed grade II

The London County Council, rebuilding the Elephant and Castle crossroads, held a competition for speculative offices on its north-east corner. This was won in 1959 by Goldfinger and the developer Arnold Lee, for whom he had worked in Albemarle Street. At the age of 56, it was his first major project.

The site had been cleared save for the Art Deco Trocadero Cinema at its southern end. Goldfinger's design set three blocks round a courtyard over car parking, all based on a 2ft 9in (0.8m) grid and the proportions of the 1:√2 rectangle. The tallest block is three times the height of the lower slabs and wider. To give variety, some bays project forwards and some are set back, with Goldfinger using the concrete soffit as a firebreak and to reflect sunlight into the interiors. In late 1960 the Ministry of Health took over the scheme, and Goldfinger revised the internal layout. The tall block contained a lift hall lined in marble, with a window of coloured glass, and the courtyard featured a pool – touches of elegance in a building designed for economy.

The new building exposed the side wall of the Trocadero, eventually demolished in 1963–64. Goldfinger completed the courtyard and built a new cinema (demolished in 1988). There was also a new Elephant and Castle public house in a small corner block, clad in grey Vitrolite to contrast with the concrete of the rest. In 2002 the offices were successfully converted to flats, during which the concrete was painted.

THE ECONOMIST GROUP

St James's Street, Westminster, London
1962–64; Alison and Peter Smithson
Listed grade II*

The Economist group is the Smithsons' masterpiece. It is barely brutalist, but a formal design of classical proportions clad in Portland stone that marked what they termed 'the shift' towards a tranquil, logical architecture intended for the client to personalise. The magazine's chairman, Geoffrey Crowther, wanted to consolidate scattered offices and build himself a penthouse flat. His deputy, Peter Dallas Smith, was persuaded to consider architects who had entered the Churchill College competition (see page 78) and with Leslie Martin narrowed his selection to Denys Lasdun and the Smithsons, whom he pitted against his friend Robin Dunn of George Trew and Dunn.

Maurice Bebb for the contractors McAlpine's suggested a low frontage block with towers behind, on a podium over service accommodation. The Smithsons' solution comprised a 17-storey block for *The Economist* behind a four-storey Martins Bank. The 18th-century Boodle's Club was given a new ladies' lounge by their assistant George Kasabov, with a narrow accommodation tower. Peter Smithson designed the elevations, the bank assuming its clean wedge shape only in July 1961, and also a double-height reception hall in Crowther's penthouse. Alison produced the other interiors (all gone), tiling the bank foyer and escalator sidings in mosaic with gold bands, repeating finishes from the competition entry for the Sydney Opera House of 1956 led by her. The complex owed something, Vincent Scully suggested, to Paul Rudolph's Blue Cross and Blue Shield building in Boston, with its bevelled corner and raised platform, and the Smithsons acknowledged Louis Kahn's Philadelphia routes in the layout.

PICCADILLY PLAZA

Piccadilly Gardens, Manchester
1962–65; Covell, Matthews & Partners

While Ralph Covell focused on church work, his partner Albert Edward 'Gerry' Matthews pursued large-scale developments through contacts made in the war. Here he collaborated with the contractor Bernard Sunley, who gave his name to the office towers. Piccadilly Plaza defines brutalism. Early drawings from 1959–61 show a crisp, curtain-walled building; then, as Ian Nairn described in *Britain's Changing Towns* (1967), 'the way which all of the parts of the Piccadilly Hotel have grown knobs since the original model appeared is a potted history of recent architectural fashion'. The long delay was notable even by the standards of the 1960s.

Built on a bomb site that had become a car park, the complex comprised three over-scaled elements on a podium. Originally with shops on two levels and from 1974 the headquarters of Piccadilly Radio, the podium forms a wall west of Piccadilly Gardens, framing the bus and tram interchange there. To the rear a broad spiral ramp accesses car parking. The hotel is further raised on cranked pilotis, with raked ends and a projecting restaurant, its fins and rooftop services the boldest elements of the design today, surviving all attempts to calm it. The 30-storey Sunley House, remodelled in 2006–07 as City Tower, still features panels by William Mitchell based on circuit boards; shallower in relief than much of his work, they were intended to be illuminated at night. The smaller office building, Bernard House, with a folded plate roof resembling a coolie hat, was rebuilt by Leslie Jones Architects in 2001–02.

STONEBOW HOUSE

The Stonebow, York
1963–65; Hartry, Grover & Halter
in succession to Wells Hickman and Partners

The Stonebow was a new street slashed through the east side of York city centre in 1955–60 and lined with modern buildings (see the Traveller pub of 1958). Many are now being replaced. The standout is Stonebow House, which fits snugly on a bowstring curve at the heart of the street, with parking for 60 cars on its roof connected by a double walkway and heated ramp. Above is a small tower, originally containing offices. The curved slab to the first floor makes a powerful statement and its concrete, with its sand-coloured aggregate, is unusually fine. Of the architects, Hartry (1920–67) and Halter (1927–2012) were Polish Jews who attended one of the two Polish schools of architecture established in Britain at the end of the war. Both were also accomplished artists.

After proposals to demolish the building were abandoned, in 2017–18 a scheme by DLA Design stripped the podium of its concrete cladding, replacing it with bronzed glass, set forward. Above, the car park was landscaped, and the offices were converted to 17 flats clad in timber and glass that continues the new bronze/gold theme within the exposed frame. A set-back additional storey accommodated four penthouses. It is a softening of the brutalist aesthetic but not a neutralisation, and the flats have been immensely successful. It proved more difficult to find an upmarket image for the ground-floor shops; nevertheless, Stonebow House might offer suggestions for the conversion and reuse of other brutalist landmarks.

RATCLIFFE-ON-SOAR POWER STATION

Nottinghamshire
1963–68; Godfrey Rossant and J. W. Gebarowicz
of Building Design Partnership

Rising demand from domestic users and industry following electricity nationalisation in 1948 saw the building of larger power stations close to supplies of water and coal. A programme planned in the late 1950s, with Derek Lovejoy as landscape architect, saw a chain of stations planned along the Trent Valley, dubbed 'Kilowatt Valley', justified by the construction of a new 400kV super-grid in 1963 and still further demand in the exceptionally cold weather in the first three months of that year. They were made possible by the success of 500MW turbines, five times the size of those built in the 1940s. Ratcliffe occupies an unusually dominant site, its tower rising above the ridge of the valley and visible across much of the Nottingham conurbation, leading to its epithet as the 'Angel of the East Midlands', situated at the meeting of the M1, River Soar and Midland Main Line.

Though based on an earlier design for Ferrybridge 'C', also by BDP, its concrete structures are more monumental than most. A metal-clad turbine hall and boiler house are lodged between eight concrete cooling towers to the classic concave design first introduced from the Netherlands in the 1920s, here set in one lozenge-shaped array. Bands of trees, mostly native species, shield low buildings and coal dumps, allowing the main buildings to shine. As of January 2022, Ratcliffe is one of only three coal-fired power stations left in the United Kingdom and will be the last when it is scheduled to close in September 2024.

SWAN HOUSE
(55 DEGREES NORTH)

Newcastle upon Tyne
1963–69; Robert Matthew, Johnson-Marshall & Partners

The A1 motorway that scythes through central Newcastle was part of the city's modernisation by the planner Wilfred Burns, brought in by the ambitious T. Dan Smith when in 1959 he became leader of Newcastle Council. Burns planned a ring of motorways around its 19th-century core, but only this one was realised. It pushed north from the Tyne Bridge of 1928 where the A1M is linked to the city street grid by a roundabout, symbolically spanned by a sentinel office block that is the centrepiece of Burns's plan. It was one of a handful of prestigious buildings commissioned by Smith from major architects, culminating in a hotel by Arne Jacobsen that was never realised.

Swan House was a commercial development originally named after Joseph Swan (1828–1914), whose pioneer experiments in electric lighting were conducted nearby. It was rechristened when in 2004 it was refurbished as a ground-floor bar and offices, flats and penthouse by Ryder HKS. Low blocks to the south and west were replaced with a 'wave' screen and fountain. Part of Burns's original brief was to rebuild the 19th-century Royal Arcade that stood on the site; this failed when the chalk numbering on the stones washed away and the concrete pastiche substituted has itself now gone. What survives is the dramatic if admittedly crude seven-storey concrete slab elevated over the road on pilotis. A conspicuous pedestrian bridge over the motorway links Swan House with the horseshoe-shaped Manors multi-storey car park of 1971 by D. T. Bradshaw, the city engineer.

ELECTRICITY SUBSTATION

Moore Street, Sheffield
1965–67; Central Electricity Generating Board
with Jefferson, Sheard & Partners
Listed grade II

Most electricity substations are low, open structures set behind a steel fence. Not so in Sheffield, identified by Ian Nairn as one of Britain's best cities for modern architecture. Electricity distribution there called for a 275-cable ring around the city centre, with transformer and switching substations to supply the local 33kV system. One of these was built as a prominent three-storey building on a long, narrow site adjoining the new ring road, replacing back-to-back housing. The electricity board demanded an uninterrupted interior for the two transformers and switchgear, with minimum heights and exceptional floor loadings, but no windows. Bryan Jefferson (1928–2014) took the opportunity to create a massive concrete structure, with an exposed frame of board-marked poured concrete designed to make the interior as open as possible. It is infilled above the ground floor with precast panels made with Cornish aggregate, intended to reduce the noise of the machinery. The ground floor is set back behind an open screen to ventilate the transformers, while the concrete parapet projects forward. Only the triangular escape tower is glazed. The internal stairs are also triangular. A second phase, at right angles, was never built.

The building began to be floodlit in 2010, switched on by Jefferson, whose practice still works in the city. It was an early indication of growing interest in brutalism, confirmed by its listing in 2013, and in 2016 it was briefly open to the public for an art exhibition. It powerfully expresses the hidden force of energy.

INSTITUTE OF CHARTERED ACCOUNTANTS

Moorgate Place, City of London
1966–70; extension, William Whitfield
Listed grade II*

John Belcher's headquarters for the Institute of Chartered Accountants of 1890–93 heralded a baroque revival, its sumptuous architecture enriched by the leading sculptors and muralists of the time. It was extended in the same style by John James Joass in 1930–31, but in 1957 the Institute amalgamated with the Society of Incorporated Accountants, bringing in 10,000 additional members. It commissioned Whitfield in 1959 to find a site for a new building but he suggested they extend their existing headquarters; adjoining properties were purchased, and the design made in 1964. Whitfield continued Joass's structure along Great Swan Alley, extending its frieze with three reliefs by David McFall, but behind and along Copthall Avenue created a nine-storey building in exposed concrete. By suspending the five new storeys of offices from beams supported on four pillars on the outside of the building, he created a great hall seating 230 for banquets without columns. Below it was a library and committee rooms, since re-purposed. Large areas of glass overcame the narrowness of the entrance hall and contrast with stainless-steel panels and the rugged, ribbed concrete of the stairs and lift towers. The result is a miniature version of Louis Kahn's Richards Medical Research Building, an influence also seen in the open concrete ceiling of the great hall. An enclosed escape stair forms the stepped corner to Langthorn Court. Whitfield also restored Belcher's principal interiors, at a time when Victorian architecture was still generally derided, finding them new uses suitable for the enlarged membership.

LEAD SHOT TOWER

Cheese Lane, Bristol
1968–69; E. N. Underwood & Partners
Listed grade II

William Watts of Bristol claimed that he had been told in a dream how to make lead shot by dropping molten lead, containing arsenic, through perforations in a piece of metal. That was in 1782, and it became the standard method of producing shot until the 1980s. Watts's own tower, near St Mary Redcliffe church, stood until 1968, when it was demolished for road widening. Every other purpose-built shot tower in England has also been demolished, except for that in Chester – and Bristol's replacement tower on a new site in St Philip's, which won a Civic Trust Award in 1969.

The Bristol Shot Tower is a remarkable example of functional concrete design, its 'Y'-shaped shaft conceived to provide the 120ft (36.6m) drop, the staircase and hoist required for the process of making lead shot. The 12-sided room at the top of the tower held the lead crucible, and – to ensure that the lead shot was not deformed by hitting the ground after its fall – there was a pool of water at the base of the tower.

The Shot Tower became redundant in the 1980s. Proposals to demolish it were delayed by the problems of decontaminating the land and aroused strong local opposition, which secured its listing in 1995. The tower was incorporated in a new office development in 2005 when the building was remodelled as a board room with a difference.

NLA HOUSE / NO.1 CROYDON

Addiscombe Road, Croydon
1968–70; Richard Seifert & Partners

A firm on the edge of brutalism, whose best buildings, as here, owe more to the rhythms and the exploitation of light and shade brought to modernism by Oscar Niemeyer. But NLA House was also the focus of a 'mini-Manhattan' of office towers built on former railway land as Croydon fought to establish its own identity separate from London. Seifert made his reputation working for developers, most notably Harry Hyams, who built extensively in Croydon with other architects. Here he realised only two – albeit very distinctive – projects, and they included one of his few buildings for a bespoke client, Noble Lowndes Annuities. This may explain the greater attention to detail and quality of finish than is often found in his work. The design capitalised on the potential of the island site, creating a 22-sided figure formed by superimposing two squares above each other, one square rotated at 45 degrees with respect to the other, and then cutting the corners off each square to form two unequal-sided octagons superimposed on each other. The effect of rotating floors and balconies produces a building that externally gives the impression of being circular, but which has office floor plans which are almost square, set over deep basements for car parking where the board-marked concrete features the NLA motif. The upper parts were originally clad in mosaic, now rendered. When new the building was popularly known as the 'Threepenny Bit' building and more recently has been compared to a stack of 50-pence pieces.

MIDLAND (NOW HSBC) BANK

Cloth Hall Street, Huddersfield
1968–70; Peter Womersley

Womersley's principal commercial building is in his home town, on the historic site of the Huddersfield Bank, the third joint-stock bank in the world when built in 1828. A replacement of 1883 proved too small for its successor, the Midland Bank, and Womersley was brought in by Roger Shaw from the executive architects Kitson, Pyman & Partners to provide a glamourous image.

The pedestrianisation of Huddersfield's main shopping street meant that Womersley was not required to splay the corner for traffic sightlines, giving the building its bold, rectangular profile. The exposed concrete is a double frame in a 'tartan' grid, i.e. pairs of columns set behind the elevations to provide space in which the services are concealed. The glazing of the banking hall is set back still further. The concrete is bushhammered and contrasted with infill panels of Brazilian old-gold granite and anodised aluminium glazing with bronze anti-solar windows. To this luxurious confection was added teak panelling and furniture in the two-storey banking hall. This has been altered, the teak has gone and a suspended ceiling added, but the internal staircase is still lined in granite and the partly set-back upper level still gives the sense of being unsupported between large areas of glass.

Womersley was raised locally and his major house, Farnley Hey, is nearby. He did realise other commercial projects, but in Hong Kong, China, where he and Walter Marmorek restored the Peninsula Hotel in 1961 and rebuilt the St George's Building (a bank and hotel) in 1965–69.

HIGH POINT

Westgate, Bradford
1970–72; John Brunton Partnership

Originally known as Permanent House, the name High Point is far more appropriate since the building stands at the highest point of Bradford's hilltop centre. It thus seems far taller than its eight storeys. It was commissioned by the Yorkshire Building Society when independent mutual societies still proudly conveyed strong local identities and Victorian solidity; with BDP's Halifax Building Society and Brunton's headquarters for the Bradford and Bingley (demolished) it marked a proud last hurrah for northern grit and self-sufficiency. High Point's ribbed concrete enforced the impression of a castle keep and the secureness of the vaults within, with glazing confined to long slits of amber float glass – then a new invention that screened solar gain and here pinkish in tone rather than bronze. The only large windows were on the fifth floor, where the senior management had their offices and boardroom. Much of the building was devoted to giant computers, which needed dark, cool spaces. The one major internal feature was William Mitchell's relief mural, 'Bradford Old and New', a smaller work than the 13 fibreglass panels he produced for the Bradford and Bingley; both works are now in storage. After the offices closed in 1997 High Point was briefly used for data storage before lying derelict for 20 years.

The Twentieth Century Society took part in a debate over High Point's future in 2018. Demolition was averted when a project to convert the building into 87 flats secured a £2.9 million grant and an elaborate transformation began in March 2021.

BERNAT KLEIN STUDIO

Near Selkirk
1970–72; Peter Womersley
Listed grade A

Peter Womersley's career switched from mid-century modernism to brutalism in the 1960s, perhaps because of repeat work from a few clients in the design world. The most famous of these was the textile innovator Bernat Klein, whose commission in 1956 for a house – High Sunderland – prompted Womersley to move to Scotland. Klein rented an 1870s lodge next door until he recalled the architect to provide a specialist studio and showroom. The brief was for a simple building costing just £25,000, which had architectural integrity and neutral colours. Integrity was a given for Womersley, but the change of palette marked a shift from High Sunderland. Whereas the house is a Miesian butterfly set amid trees, The Studio is a bold roadside statement inspired by Frank Lloyd Wright's Fallingwater, which Womersley considered 'the most beautiful house I know', though he never visited it.

The temple-like structure has a brick plinth and a brick core containing services. Four columns support the main first-floor studio, with twin mullions carrying the roof. A first-floor bridge eased Klein's stroll down the hill from High Sunderland and provided a fire escape, permitting the open interior. Precast edge beams project beyond the end elevations, where mild steel upstands form a visual extension of the windows above. With no corner glazing bars to the Crittall glazing, the stepped, horizontal levels appear to float amid the woodland.

TRANSPORT

LEE CIRCLE CAR PARK

Lee Street, Leicester
1961; Fitzroy Robinson & Partners

The Leicester 'Multidek', subsequently known as the Auto-Magic Car Park, was one of the first large multi-storey car parks in Europe, the very names redolent of its era. It seems bigger because it stands on a raised island of land surrounded by roads. The continuous double-spiral ramps, engineered by C. G. Mander & Partners and erected by Bison (specialists in prefabricated concrete), serve spaces for 1,047 cars on six levels. The result combines a look of Fiat's Lingotto factory with the Chateau de Chambord, the best historic example of interleaved floors and double-helix ramps. Here the helix ramps divide the parking in two, colour-coded red and blue, linked only at top and bottom. The Multidek was also among the first car parks to be automated, with coin-operated barriers.

Beneath the six storeys of parking, there was a forecourt petrol station and automated car wash. Better still, in the ground floor and basement Tesco launched a 'wonder store', their first supermarket outside the Home Counties. Opened by Sid James from *Hancock's Half Hour* and the *Carry On* films in December 1961, it claimed to be the largest supermarket in Europe, with household goods as well as groceries laid out on a self-service plan. Staff were on hand to take customers' purchases direct to their cars. There was also a 36-lane ten-pin bowling alley – an American craze that swept across Britain in 1961.

NCP   Welcome to Lee Circle Car Park   P

Direct Fabric Warehouse

Material Magic

NCP
P
Lee Circle Car Park

P
NCP

LANCASTER (FORMERLY FORTON) SERVICES, M6

Bay Horse, Lancashire
1964–65; Bill Galloway and Ray Anderson of T. P. Bennett & Sons
Listed grade II

Motorways symbolised Britain's technological, cultural and economic progress in the decade 1955–65 and the service station was its most direct expression. Nowhere took up the challenge like Lancashire County Council, as a means of linking its long, narrow area to itself and to London. The first parts of the M6 to be built, in 1956–59, were bypasses for Preston and Lancaster.

Service areas were initially provided at 24-mile (39km) intervals. The only models were the stations on the Italian *autostrade* and American parkways, which often stretched across the carriageways. The Ministry of Transport set out the basic site layouts and general rules for a 24-hour service without alcohol. In the mid-60s the all-night cappuccino bar was an attractive prospect, although the most ambitious of the early service stations aimed at something more stylish. Designs were vetted by the ministry, local authorities and the Royal Fine Art Commission. Forton's special feature was its views towards the Lake District and Morecambe Bay, so restaurant-goers could combine the excitement of speed with splendid sunsets. A waiter-service restaurant – with 120 covers – was built in a tower, originally intended to be 100ft (30.5m) high but chopped to 65ft (20m) by the planners. The octagonal shape resembled that of airport control towers. It closed in 1989, partly as a result of the cost of meeting current fire-escape regulations, and has since become offices.

NEW STREET SIGNAL BOX

Birmingham
1964–66; Bicknell and Hamilton, assisted by Diana Quin
Listed grade II

John Bicknell and Paul Hamilton had designed Harlow station and many signal boxes for British Railways before setting up their own practice in 1963. The electrification of the Euston line included automatically locking signals, requiring signal boxes with more power. Birmingham controls 350 signals and over 220 points; then the largest signal box in Britain, it was also the first multi-storey box on a central city site. The setting has been radically altered by the removal of adjacent buildings and the construction of an elevated road alongside.

The accommodation is laid out on five levels around a central shaft projecting above the roof. The top-floor control room is surrounded by a deep, cantilevered fascia to shade the console from the sun. The technical brief demanded heavy floor loadings and exceptional sound insulation, while sensitive electronic equipment had to be shielded by blank walls. The reinforced concrete structure, based on a 10ft x 20ft (3m x 6m) grid, comprises pre-stressed floor slabs with beams and columns round a central service core. The cladding is exposed aggregate precast concrete units with a triangular profile to give a corrugated effect, chosen because of the tight site and restricted access. Hamilton felt that the prominent location demanded a formal expression of its purpose, reflecting its importance and much tougher than their earlier buildings, though he also likened the completed signal box to a 'log house'.

BUS STATION AND CAR PARK

Tithebarn Street, Preston
1968–69; Keith Ingham and Charles Wilson, Building Design Partnership
Listed grade II

Brutalism's greatest conservation success, a landmark equal to the great Victorian library and museum nearby. Central Preston was a bottleneck, thanks to its bus stands and exacerbated by long-distance coaches following the opening of the M6. The corporation commissioned a bus station and multi-storey car park for 500 vehicles as early as 1959 but in 1966, when the town was set to become part of the Central Lancashire New Town, it revived its plans and commissioned a building doubled in size. On opening it was the largest bus station in Europe. Its closest comparison is with Paul Rudolph's Temple Street car park in New Haven of 1959–62, but Ingham and Wilson made their structure lighter and more elegant by using fibreglass moulds. They used the same German material, Glaskon Glasfilme, for the bold signage, telephone kiosks and timetable holders. The result is a series of upswept balustrades to the split-level car parking, four on the west side and five on the east, accessed by external ramps at either end, with a taxi rank to the south. There were originally 40 bus stands on either side, but the restoration by John Puttick Associates with Cassidy + Ashton has relocated all the buses to the east side, securing a greater connection with the town by creating an open plaza to the west. Care has also been taken to restore the interior of the bus station with its oiled iroko finishes, intended by Ingham to give 'something like airport standards' to travellers by bus.

KINGSWAY TUNNEL VENTILATION SHAFTS

Liverpool and Wallasey
1968–71; Thomas Harker of Bradshaw, Rowse & Harker

Liverpool's first Mersey Tunnel, opened in 1934, combined Basil Mott's novel engineering with Herbert Rowse's sophisticated Art Deco. Their successor practices were charged in 1966 to build a second and wider pair of tunnels a mile to the north, linking to the future M53 in response to growing traffic congestion, after a design for a suspension bridge was rejected. A test shaft was bored manually, but then the first tunnel and related ventilation ducts were realised in three years using a massive mechanical borer imported from Pakistan and nicknamed the 'Mersey Mole'.

This time there were two, not six, ventilation shafts and there was no attempt to hide their function. Harker first proposed two circular vents flanking a circular chimney resembling a cooling tower, but the design was dismissed as too outrageous. The plan was retained but within it the elements became more rectilinear. The air intakes to either side look like intakes, with efficient horizontal fans rather than the awkward vertical units used in the 1930s, while the chimney looks like a chimney, but these elements have been exaggerated into something more powerful and personalised, almost animal-like, the ventilators tapering inwards like contemporary radio sets and the chimney swelling outwards as it rises and braced like a rocket poised for blast-off.

INDEX

All photographs © Elain Harwood, except the following: page 14 Martin Bond/Alamy; 16 Washington Imaging/Alamy; 27 James O. Davies/ Historic England; 54–55 Galit Seligmann/Alamy; 59 Arcaid Images/Alamy; 62–63 Simon Turner/Alamy; 90–91 FocusEurope/Alamy; 98–99 Clearview/Alamy; 100–101 Robert Evans/Alamy; 118–119 Nathaniel Noir/Alamy; 142 Paul Adams/Alamy; 152–153 KBImages/ Alamy; 190 Sally-Ann Norman-VIEW/Alamy; 204–205 Brian Anthony/Alamy; 219 Architectural Press Archive/RIBA Collections; 232 lovethephoto/Alamy; 254–255 Steve Taylor ARPS/Alamy; 258–259 Richard Naude/Alamy; 260–261 Paul Weston/Alamy; 292–293 Alex Ramsay/Alamy; 296–297 Paul Adams-North West Images/Alamy